Arianna,

Best wishes,

Myrna.

May 14' '14

When Talent Goes Global:

What CEOs, Boards and Management Teams
Must Learn and Do to Win With a Diverse, Global Workforce

by Uzma S. Burki

Library of Congress Cataloging-in-Publication Data

Burki, Uzma S.
    When talent goes global: what CEOs, boards and management teams must learn and do to win with a diverse, global workforce / Uzma S. Burki
    Includes bibliographical references.
    ISBN - 13: 978-0615966014
    ISBN - 10: 0615966012

Dedicated

to the loving memory of my dear parents

CONTENTS

FOREWORD

by Kevin Oakes, CEO, i4cp

I remember the conversation vividly. I was talking with the Chief Human Resource Officer of a very large, global consumer products company. This company has close to 200,000 employees, operates in almost 200 countries, and is headquartered in Europe, but their products are known to people almost anywhere in the world. I was attempting to get this company to join membership to my organization, the Institute for Corporate Productivity, and to take advantage of the research and peer networking we provide. The conversation was going reasonably well until he made a simple statement:

"Kevin, how truly global are the companies in your network?"

When I went on to describe some of the global organizations, he quickly stopped me. He wanted "truly global" companies, not companies that have their executive team made up primarily of people residing in one country, look at one country as their primary market and the rest of the world as "emerging" or "growth opportunities," and staff those countries with expatriates. He meant a company that looks at itself as not being anchored by one culture or political structure — a company that views the world as an equal opportunity market and customer base.

I had to admit that I couldn't think of any that viewed themselves this way. And then I realized there probably aren't many companies *anywhere* that view themselves this way.

This particular company's teams are truly spread out around the world. Various countries are top revenue producers, and the CEO spends most of his time on the road. The diversity of the leadership and the employee base is unmatched, and one word very clearly dominates their website, literature and investor materials: global.

Today, most large organizations recruit from worldwide talent pools, buy from worldwide vendors, sell to worldwide customers and distribute through worldwide channels. Yet too many still act like dynasties of yore: the King operates from the castle back home and the explorers are out conquering distant lands. That needs to change, and it's clear from my company's research that "global-mindedness" is no longer an option; it is a given for high-performance organizations (HPOs).

Let me explain what I mean by an HPO, because our research centers almost exclusively on this characteristic. HPOs are organizations that, over the last five years, have outperformed the competition in four key categories: revenue growth, profitability, market share and customer satisfaction. As we research the people practices of companies, we delineate high-performance organizations (HPOs) from low-performance organizations (LPOs). The differences are often startling.

For example, an i4cp study titled *High-Performance Global Staffing: Shifting Labor Supplies and Strategies*, found that LPOs are five times more likely than HPOs (30% to 6%) to staff management positions in a different country exclusively with expatriates from the organization's headquarters. Almost half of HPOs say they prefer to use a mix of expats along with local hires.

The study shines a light on corporate global expansion and how top companies approach it. Ninety-three percent of respondents say that their company will maintain or increase global staffing within the next three years. As opposed to just maintaining global staffing, 60% of all companies polled indicated they expect some expansion of their global workforce in the next three years. For high-performance organizations, this number jumps to 74%. As organizations grow globally, it's only natural that global leadership development takes on more importance.

Developing global leaders is an issue that perplexes most companies however, whether they are high or low performing. Our research shows that HPOs are tackling the challenges of global leadership development through a combination of broader thinking, deeper analysis, and higher expectations. The fourth annual i4cp/AMA/*Training* magazine study of challenges and opportunities in global leadership development highlight four next practices among its key findings:

1. **There is a shift to defining leaders by influence, not role.** More than half of HPOs define leaders not by their position on the organization chart but by their degree of

influence and performance. With flatter, more matrixed organizations, employees are discovering they need leadership skills to collaborate with colleagues in another business unit, share expertise with peers in a different geographic location or work on ad-hoc projects.

2. **HPOs are allowing managers to self-select involvement in global leadership development programs.** While C-suite executives and high-potential employees are still prime targets for global leadership development, making the process available to any manager who expresses interest in it sets HPOs apart from LPOs. Further, it is a practice that correlates to global leadership development effectiveness, one of the dependent variables analyzed in the study.

3. **Strategic workforce planning (SWP) is playing a pivotal role in driving the content of global leadership development processes.** Long-term strategies and values continue to influence global leadership development, but our research finds increased emphasis on using SWP to identify competency gaps and drive the content of global leadership development. Nearly twice as many HPOs as LPOs use strategic workforce planning in this manner, and it's a practice that significantly correlates to global leadership development effectiveness.

4. **Business performance is gaining prominence as a measure of global leadership development effectiveness.** Although emphasis on standard measures such as participant satisfaction and behavioral changes continues, we have found a rise in the use of measures such as sales and productivity compared with previous iterations. Engagement scores of the leaders' direct reports have also seen an uptick as a measure, and this is correlated to global leadership development effectiveness.

These next practices are a blueprint for companies that want to elevate their global leadership development practices to emulate those of HPOs.

When looking below the leadership line there is a fairly large disparity between high- and low-performing organizations in how they deal with technically skilled employees. Forty-one percent of HPOs prefer to assign technically skilled employees regardless of where they were recruited, while a mere 18% of LPOs say the same. Also, HPOs are much less likely to move people from their home country to a foreign headquarters (or some other hub). Only 10% of HPOs say they do this, compared to 24% of LPOs.

All of this brings to light the importance of diversity in the workforce, a trait that separates globally-ready companies from the rest. Research shows that there is a correlation between the number of women in senior management positions and improved corporate performance, and yet just 4% of CEOs of U.S. companies are women. Multiple studies conducted by Catalyst have established an empirical link between gender diversity in corporate leadership and financial performance, including an oft-cited study finding that Fortune 500 companies with high percentages of female officers had a 35% higher return on equity and a 34% higher total return to shareholders than companies with fewer women executives.[1]

McKinsey & Company has noted as part of its *Women Matter* research that "companies benefit from the different but complementary leadership styles that women bring to their work, to the extent that there is a link between the proportion of women in senior management positions and corporate performance."[2]

Globally, progress is painfully slow in the numbers of women being elevated to senior management positions in most parts of the world: Women account for just 17% of seats on corporate boards and 10% of executive committees in Europe. In the U.S. it's just as bad; women account for 15% of seats on corporate boards and 14% of executive

---

[1] "The Bottom Line: Connecting Corporate Performance and Gender Diversity." Catalyst. New York: 2004

[2] Quoted in "Women Matter: An Asian Perspective." Original source: Women Matter 2010: "Women at the top of corporations: Making it happen." McKinsey & Company: 2012.

committees.[3] Recent steps forward seem to be fueled largely by concern about worsening talent shortages in some regions, especially in Asia, where corporations have been very slow in opening the C-suite to women.

A 2013 article in *The New York Times* reported that Asian universities are beginning to follow the lead of business schools such as Harvard and Stanford in offering specialized programs to develop female business leaders. For example, the University of Hong Kong recently launched a program designed to prepare Asian women for the boardroom. Similar initiatives and special courses for female executives are offered at the Indian Institute of Management Bangalore, Peking University, and the National University of Singapore. In the article, Dr. Vivian Lim, director of the National University of Singapore's Women in Leadership program, noted that the growth of such programs in Asia is in response to challenges presented by critical talent shortages in the region: "Organizations have come to realize that women provide a ready pool of talent and more can be done to harness this reserve of talents."[4]

In addition to gender diversity, HPOs have consistently viewed diversity initiatives differently than their low-performance brethren. In i4cp's *12 Diversity Practices of High Performance Organizations* report, we found that top organizations:

1. Are more likely to build the business case for diversity on the need to reflect their customer base and community demographics
2. Make diversity an important consideration in developing their succession plan
3. Place more importance on framing diversity as a business relevant issue and on creating accountability
4. Have a more inclusive definition of diversity

---

[3] Chart used in "Women Matter: An Asian Perspective." Original source: McKinsey proprietary database, 2011. McKinsey & Company: 2012.

[4] Yang, Calvin. "Asian Universities Offer Programs for Female Business Leaders." *The New York Times*: May 27, 2013.

5. Are less likely than lower performers to sponsor employee resource groups that are based on traditional diversity labels or categories
6. Are more likely to specifically budget for diversity initiatives
7. Are more likely to assign responsibility for leading and executing the diversity strategy to the executive team
8. Place greater emphasis on diversity recruiting and are more likely to concentrate training on diversity skills
9. Do not attempt to calculate the ROI of their diversity investments
10. Monitor diversity success by looking at both their applicant pools and their ability to retain once the talent is in the door
11. Are less likely than lower performers to compare diversity metrics against minority representation in the community
12. Are more likely to conduct an annual CEO review and to tie results to compensation

Diversity often goes hand-in-hand with inclusiveness in an organization. When reviewing diversity and inclusion, measurement is an important component, and most diversity professionals will assert that they have a handle on diversity metrics, which are tricky but relatively clear-cut measurements and groupings around identifiable or discoverable traits. It doesn't matter whether those traits are race and gender or education and experience — they are elements that can be classified and quantified.

However, the inclusiveness of an organization's culture can be harder to pin down. It's difficult to report that the company is now 5% more inclusive, or try to quantify what effect that statement has on the bottom line.

In the absence of direct measures, it's often necessary to rely on indirect observation to determine if goals are being achieved. Metrics such as engagement scores, retention rates, productivity measures and diversity representation at various tiers must often be combined to create a broader picture of an inclusion strategy's impact on the overall organizational culture.

In its *Inclusion Measurement Policies and Practices Report*, i4cp found distinct characteristics of top organizations when it came to measuring inclusion:

- HPOs are over three times more likely to analyze the link between inclusion and productivity
- In support of their talent acquisition and employment brand, HPOs are three times more likely to cite participation in third-party "employer of choice" lists as a driver of inclusion initiatives
- HPOs make a point of supporting branding efforts by including inclusion-specific messaging on websites and in other communications
- HPOs have an internal champion at the executive level who promotes the success of an inclusion strategy
- HPOs hold managers accountable for inclusion-specific goals
- While inclusion in some form is part of most organizations' people strategy, HPOs are more likely to have it as a talent management function separate from diversity

As companies recognize the importance of the talent necessary to compete in a global marketplace, they also recognize that developing global leaders and creating a diverse workforce is the product of a culture and mindset centered on universal global competencies. Although some key components of global talent development have remained steady over the past few years, the business environment is anything but status quo. ***When Talent Goes Global*** rightly makes the case that a more progressive recognition of what is required to work beyond borders is essential. **The companies that master this will truly achieve and sustain high performance.**

INTRODUCTION

Consistently high-performing organizations inevitably have senior executives, boards, and management teams that are adept at anticipating and responding to changes in their industry. Whether technological advances, shifts in market demands, regulatory changes, or other variables, an ability to adapt quickly and effectively is a competitive necessity for 21st century businesses.

Today's most critical "change" challenges often center on the increasingly global nature of doing business. The realities of globalization are no longer limited to the largest multinational corporations. Even relatively small companies in most industries are now expanding (or should be) into international markets, maintaining or developing global supply chains, and seeking more effective ways to outperform competitors from other nations.

Many strategic issues involving globalization receive well-deserved attention among executives and industry groups, in MBA programs, and in the business media. But one issue is too often pushed into the background or insufficiently understood: the globalization of talent and related diversification of the workforce.

My own background — as a foreign national who came to the U.S. for graduate school, a Fortune 500 HR executive, and a consultant specializing in human capital, including cultural integration and talent management — has given me ample opportunity to see both the challenges presented by a global workforce and its extraordinary potential as a competitive differentiator. Indeed, much of my career has been spent helping executives like you to overcome those challenges and realize that potential — and that is also my purpose in writing this book.

U.S.-based executives in particular are experiencing a complex set of workforce changes that led me to feel that a book exploring a new talent paradigm was urgently needed. These changes are occurring *within* the U.S. workforce as well as resulting from the addition of regional operations in other countries, leading to outsourcing and the increased mobility, accessibility, and strategic value of global talent.

We'll examine the demographic and cultural realities of these changes throughout the book. But even without delving into the statistics, as we'll do in Chapter 1, you are probably already keenly aware that the U.S. workforce has undergone, and continues to undergo, significant transformation. Indigenous demographic changes, as well as trends involving immigration, worker migration, gender and ethnic differences, sexual orientation, and more, have made the U.S. labor force undeniably older, more racially and ethnically diverse, more female, and inclusive of more groups demanding fair and equal treatment.

A second reason it is essential to address the issues explored in this book involves the impact of globalization in general. It is well understood that global business opportunities raise new challenges in terms of integrating parent and affiliate operations, managing global trade risks, deploying appropriate technology, and understanding differences in other nations' (or international) laws. Similarly, executives must become attuned not only to the opportunities afforded by global operations and recruitment of global talent, but also to the new challenges that must be managed to do so successfully.

Yes, "going global" can help you acquire high-skill individuals whose technical knowledge can give you a competitive edge; it can also be a way to reduce labor costs in low-skill operations. But you won't achieve these advantages if your organization doesn't make the adaptations necessary to retain, develop, manage, and ensure the productivity of people from other cultures.

For example, consider the rise of the BRIC nations (Brazil, Russia, India, and China). The aggregate GDP (gross domestic product) of BRIC countries quadrupled during the first decade of the 21st century, from $3 trillion to close to $12 trillion — and some estimates have the BRIC economies overtaking the G7 (U.S., U.K., Canada, Germany, France, Japan and Italy) as early as 2027.[5]

---

[5] O'Neill, Jim. **The Growth Map: Economic Opportunity in the BRICs and Beyond**. Penguin Group, New York, NY: 2011.

The significance here is twofold. First, companies in BRIC nations with flexible supply chains have become formidable competitors, even against established market leaders with powerful brands, solid customer loyalty, and deep resources. Many of these aggressive new competitors are government-backed companies with access to lower-cost capital. This has shifted the competitive terrain. Where companies once competed primarily on products and services, not processes, they must now compete on the strength of their supply chains. Companies in the U.S. can no longer "go it alone" and expect success. They must collaborate with the right partners to increase speed, promote innovation, and gain market share. That includes tapping the power of global talent that increasingly involves workers, offshore vendors, supply chain partners, and customers *from* BRIC nations.

The challenge is cultural as much as operational. For example, as we'll see in Chapter 3, BRIC nations tend to have a "collectivist" orientation, while the U.S. is an "individualist" culture. To capitalize on BRIC talent, and compete effectively in these nations, it is necessary to understand and bridge such cultural differences. Further, BRIC is just the most notable emerging block. Another on the horizon is MINT (Malaysia, Indonesia, Nigeria and Turkey). Still others are emerging or will emerge as part of increased global economic interdependence — new forces for U.S. corporations to contend with as economic competitors, and as both sources of, and competitors for, talent.

Increased interdependence of the world's economies, and increased competition across the board, mean that U.S. corporations must seize every possible advantage, including getting more out of a global workforce. Those that already have an established global business footprint, and understand the value and challenges of diversity from their existing workforce, are well-positioned to leverage what I call the diversity formula: Employees + Supply Chain + Customers = Competitive Advantage. However, the truth is that almost *all* businesses will need to tap into a broader array of talent power centers to remain competitive.

As an executive, you probably have noticed that your talent pool looks very different than it did in the 1990s — or even a decade ago. The demographics make it clear that it will look even more different in the years ahead. Your workforce will become more multicultural, include more women, see Baby Boomers replaced by Millennials, and likely involve more people who identify as LGBT as well. Now is the time to assess what you need to do to better attract, retain, and manage that talent pool.

The changing workforce demographics I have described above are accompanied by sociological and cultural changes and new attitudes about workplace relationships. Unfortunately, many companies focus almost exclusively on demographic issues like recruiting, without fully addressing the need to adapt development and promotion strategies, management styles, and other areas to these shifting values. Diversity of human capital can be extremely valuable, but it requires both a depth of commitment and a breadth of managerial activity that remains rare.

That rarity creates an outstanding competitive opportunity. Organizations taking the extra steps to manage diverse, global talent well are gaining a real edge. This book can help executives like you take those steps — from confronting past stereotypes and adopting a new talent paradigm to developing and implementing strategies to better communicate with and motivate multicultural talent. Among other issues, I especially want to emphasize how understanding and respecting the different values and mindsets of employees from other cultures can open the door to greater creativity, innovation, and overall performance *from* those employees.

* * * * *

As noted earlier, I bring a unique perspective to this subject. First, I am part of the "global talent" that more and more companies are seeing in their workforce. I speak from a lifetime of experience straddling different national, regional, and corporate cultures.

I was born, raised, and initially educated in Pakistan, a community-oriented society with Eastern values and traditions. After much debate, and my winning a scholarship, I convinced my family that I should come to the U.S. to further my education, earning graduate degrees from Kansas State University, the Fletcher School of Law and Diplomacy – Tufts University, and Columbia. I then began my career with U.S.-based Citibank in Pakistan as a banker serving emerging markets. Later I became the first female transferred from Pakistan to the U.S. — this time as a human capital professional.

INTRODUCTION

In a real sense, I am an example of diversity succeeding on both the individual and organizational level. I know from experience what enabled me to develop as a professional, rise into leadership, and contribute to the fullest of my potential. I also know where cultural "blind spots" tended to create obstacles for people like me.

I've spent many years on the organizational side of the relationship too. Since arriving in the U.S. in the 1990s, I have held executive management positions involving both strategic and operational responsibilities for multicultural workforces:

- Vice President of Employee Development, Knowledge Management and Training at Citibank
- Senior Vice President of Retail Performance and Development for National City Bank
- Chief Learning and Organizational Development Officer and Human Resources Strategist with Ameriprise Financial
- Head of Human Resources, Vice President for Biomedical Services at the American Red Cross, where I provided support to 20,000+ employees and managed a staff of 225
- Head of HC Strategy, Talent Development, Talent Acquisition, Risk Management, Training, Analytics and Change Management at Amtrak, leading a team of 117 people and supporting a diverse workforce of 20,000+ employees

In these positions, I had direct reports from many different cultural backgrounds, and was deeply involved in talent identification and acquisition, labor relations, employee relations, professional development, HR policies and procedures, diversity and inclusion initiatives, and other critical areas. My experiences showed me how absolutely vital it is for executives to "get it right" when managing a diverse, global workforce. As a "cultural outsider" who had an insider's understanding of organizational dynamics and strategic objectives, I also saw that I could offer unique insights and guidance to help such executives. To do so, I founded Altvia Consulting, a firm specializing in cultural integration, talent management and development, and related change management.

Through it all, I have seen again and again that the strength of an organization's human capital is a key determinant in whether it is one of its industry's high performers, average, or an underperformer.

Like most executives — and the research-based Institute for Corporate Productivity (i4cp) — I define high-performing organizations as those that consistently outperform competitors in revenue growth, market share, profitability, and customer satisfaction. Increasingly, that requires a leadership team that has the global mindset, emotional agility, and cultural intelligence to effectively manage and motivate a diverse, global workforce. Like my consulting work, this book is designed to give executives a better grasp of the cultural underpinnings of that workforce and illuminate a path toward more successful strategies for development, engagement, and retention of diverse talent. There are four core areas that merit attention in this regard:

- Aligning your human capital strategy to business strategy
- Assessing supply and demand relative to the business's strategic workforce planning (environmental scanning)
- Developing and managing talent strategy around the business model specific to regional and global business realities — i.e., one size does *not* fit all
- Acquiring talent that is the "best fit" overall, including compatibility and/or complementarity with the organizational culture, rather than focusing only on technical competence, etc.

Much of what I cover in this book has a direct impact on these four core areas. In that respect, it is especially valuable for senior and C-level executives to read *before* revisiting top-level objectives and business strategies — because, ultimately, the success of any strategy requires getting the most out of your human capital.

Uzma S. Burki, Owner
Altvia Consulting, LLC
March 2014

PART I

The Need for a Global Talent Paradigm — and How to Get There

Business expansion driven by globalization — of markets, supply chains, and the workforce — creates real opportunities, as well as real management challenges, for today's business leaders. Prospering in this globally integrated environment requires adapting and constantly refining business strategies, including talent strategy. Indeed, as globalization helps push talent to the foreground as an organizational stakeholder and competitive differentiator, it is becoming imperative for executives to develop a global mindset toward talent. Those who tailor talent strategies based on an understanding of global talent, and align organizational activities accordingly, will put their companies on the crest of the next wave of growth. Those who don't do so will be at a serious disadvantage and may not survive the sea change.

For more than a decade, I have worked in a range of roles to help executives develop and implement strategies that align with global realities. In an increasingly global economy, that work is more important than ever, particularly in the area of talent. Demographic trends in immigration, worker migration, gender, ethnicity, and age all continue to dramatically alter the composition of the workforce. Moreover, there is a growing demand from all groups for equal rights, not just legally but in terms of day-to-day inclusion and respect. Managing this diverse, global workforce creates some of the most impactful challenges that leaders and management teams can face.

As an executive — and a non-U.S. native who has spent her career negotiating the intersection of two national cultures and varying organizational cultures — I empathize with those struggling to overcome these challenges. But to succeed, we have to be clear on one point: The "problems" do not stem from the new workforce's heterogeneity, but

23

rather from the inability of managers to fully comprehend its dynamics, divest themselves of prejudicial attitudes, and devise new ways to more effectively tap the incredible potential of diverse groups.

In today's marketplace, there are ample incentives — of both the stick and the carrot variety — for executives to move diversity, inclusion, and talent management to the top of the strategic agenda. On the "stick" side, companies unable or unwilling to change their policies and practices are likely to suffer serious consequences:

- Intergroup conflicts among employees, impacting productivity, morale, and teamwork
- Limited or lost access to the growing pool of talented employees (and potential leaders) from other cultures
- Vulnerability to high-profile lawsuits that are costly to defend and settle, and can damage public reputation, brand value, and even access to capital
- Missed opportunities to form valuable business partnerships and alliances

The good news is that there are also attractive payoffs for forward-thinking leaders who make a concerted effort to adapt their mindset and their organizations to better align with a multicultural workforce:

- Attracting and retaining the best available talent regardless of culture, birthplace, age, gender, or sexual orientation
- Improved individual and organizational productivity
- Integration of fresh perspectives, spurring innovation and more effective problem-solving
- Greater flexibility throughout the culture
- New paths to expand into global markets as well as gain market share locally
- Higher quality of management
- Brand differentiation as a corporate citizen known for being socially responsible

I will examine these benefits, and how to realize them, throughout the book. Here I just want to emphasize that being able to successfully manage a multicultural workforce is no longer a "nice to have" reserved for a few select organizations. Yes, it is one of the hallmarks of high-performing organizations, but even companies with less lofty aspirations must confront the hard reality that the value you get, or fail to get, from your multicultural workforce directly impacts your bottom line. Leveraging diverse, global talent should be on everyone's list of strategic priorities — not only because it's the right thing to do from a humanistic standpoint, but also because it will help your business reduce costs and increase profits.

Globalization will continue to have a profound impact on all aspects of business. Prospering in this increasingly connected world requires executives like you to lead the way by demonstrating flexibility, respect for cultural differences, and sometimes new or even unconventional approaches to management.

In this section of the book, we'll help you on that journey by first defining important workforce and population trends and newly emerging talent centers in Chapter 1. Next, Chapter 2 will look at the agility and "global mindset" that will enable executives to deal more effectively with the changing talent pool. In Chapter 3, we'll explore the need to challenge stereotypes and develop a deeper understanding of cultural differences. To close this section, Chapter 4 will explain why merely assembling a diverse workforce is not enough, and then lay out the principles to achieve a truly inclusive environment that yields higher performance, not just a wider range of differences.

CHAPTER 1

Demographic Trends and
Newly Emerging Talent Centers

The enterprise of the past was most often defined by what it owned: manufacturing sites, inventory, fixed and liquid assets, and so on. For very large organizations, such assets required huge investments that usually went beyond the capacity of any individual or group of individuals. As a result, many enterprises came to be owned, and to varying degrees controlled, by their investors and shareholders.

In contrast, today's enterprises are as likely to be defined by the value provided by their human capital as by the value of their plants and machines. Changes in financial markets have also made it easier to finance large investments, so capital intensity is no longer as critical. In short, gaining a competitive edge in today's marketplace is increasingly about specialized human capital driving new innovations, better business processes, and sometimes even creating entirely new markets.

With an enterprise's workforce becoming an increasingly vital source of its value and profitability, there is added pressure on executives to meet the challenges of managing and developing talent. But that's more complex than it was in the past. Today's enterprise is almost never a stable entity with a homogeneous talent pool. Many have operations in multiple countries. But even among those operating primarily or exclusively in the U.S., the reality is that most organizations are comprised of myriad subcultures, with employees coming from a diverse range of backgrounds.

In order to get the most out of this new workforce, it is helpful to understand the trends shaping it. It is also important to be cognizant of the newly emerging talent centers that increasingly will be the source of the employees who determine your organization's success or failure. For most companies, that future success will depend to a large extent on how well they can attract, develop, and retain people from these talent centers.

Global Workforce Trends

Major global workforce trends are influencing organizations and markets everywhere — but their impact is especially notable on the U.S. as the world's largest and most developed economy. Whether your organization is already recruiting and developing global talent, or simply confronting what a global workforce is doing for your competitors, no one can afford to ignore the larger trends shaping the availability and nature of today's human capital. Few industries or organizations will be untouched by the rapidly evolving realities of the global workforce. Thus, even if your current situation tempts you to say, "This doesn't effect us," the better approach is to assume it *will*, and look for the best ways to turn it to your advantage.

Identifying global workforce trends, understanding which trends will accelerate in the years ahead, and grasping the challenges and opportunities inherent in these trends lays the foundation for developing a global workforce strategy that will help you leverage the forces in your favor. Naturally, which trends merit your fullest attention will depend on your specific industry and organization. That level of understanding and planning is the scope of a consulting engagement rather than a book, so here I just want to provide a 30,000-foot view of the workforce trend terrain.

Expansion of Global Economic Trade

In both manufacturing and service sectors, lower barriers to entry, technological connectivity, and other forces are making it feasible for more and more companies to compete in, and source supplies from, markets all over the world. This is having a direct impact on the flow of labor as well. On both the individual talent and the human capital (HC) sides of the equation, there is greater knowledge of opportunities beyond the immediate locale. Add in increased population mobility, and the end result for corporations is a rapidly expanding, and diversifying, talent pool. From a competitive standpoint, recruiting the "best and brightest" truly requires a global approach.

Population Shifts

Despite projected growth in the global population from 6.9 billion in 2010 to 7.6 billion in 2020, the working-age population is expected to decline in many countries, including the U.S., Italy, Japan, China, and Russia.[6] Emerging market economies with younger labor forces, such as Brazil, Mexico, India, and Indonesia, may gain a demographic "dividend" through the surge in productivity and growth associated with an expanding labor pool. As it becomes more difficult for a country like the U.S. to meet all its labor needs via its native-born population, it will become important to be able to draw workers from these emerging marketing economies to remain competitive.

Rapid Emergence of BRIC

Taken together, Brazil, Russia, India, and China (BRIC) make up more than 40% of the world's population. Jim O'Neill, global economist at Goldman Sachs, suggests that BRIC's economic potential is such that they could be among the four most dominant economies by 2050.[7] These countries encompass over 25% of the world's land coverage and 40% of the world's population, and hold a combined GDP (PPP) of $20 trillion.[8] On almost every scale, they constitute the largest entity on the global stage, and are among the largest and fastest-growing emerging markets. These nations, and the organizations headquartered there, are becoming formidable competitors, with repercussions throughout the global economy. An increasingly well-trained workforce in BRIC nations

---

[6] "Tracking Global Trends: How Six Key Developments Are Shaping the Business World." Published online at www.ey.com/GL/en/Issues/Business-environment/Six-global-trends-shaping-the-business-world---Demographic-shifts-transform-the-global-workforce. EYGM Limited: 2011.

[7] "Interview with Jim O'Neill." *Financial Times*, November 6, 2006.

[8] "BRIC." Published online at: en.wikipedia.org/wiki/BRIC. Wikipedia: 2014.

is a vital part of their growth, but this workforce is also mobile. Competing for the "best and brightest" from these countries is becoming a key front in the battle for global economic power. As mentioned in my Introduction to this book, BRIC is just one of the emerging blocks to consider, with MINT (Malaysia, Indonesia, Nigeria, Turkey) being another notable rising force in the global marketplace.

Outsourcing/Offshoring

For both manufacturing and service-oriented jobs, more and more companies are leveraging the advantages of a global workforce through outsourcing and offshoring. In the U.S., there has been some backlash against this politically and in terms of customer satisfaction (e.g., complaints about service calls routed to non-U.S. reps with hard-to-understand accents). However, the advantages are too significant to imagine a future where outsourcing/offshoring will become less common. The competitive distinction will not be which companies employ or eschew the practice, but rather which companies make the *wisest* use of it.

Women on the Rise

Women now represent 40% of the global labor force (World Bank, 2011), with the Female Labor Force Participation Rate (FLPR) hovering around 50% over the past two decades. The average gender participation gap — the difference between male and female labor force participation rates — has been declining since 1990, largely due to a worldwide fall in male labor force participation rates, but it remains significant.[9] Nevertheless, most countries are seeing increasing numbers of women enter, and remain in, the workforce, and the gender participation gap *has* narrowed in most regions,[10] with women's share growing significantly in

---

[9] Elborgh-Woytek, Katrin; Monique Newiak; Kalpana Kochhar; Stefania Fabrizio; Kangni Kpodar; Philippe Wingender; Benedict Clements; and Gerd Schwartz. **Women, Work and the Economy: Macroeconomic Gains from Gender Equity**. International Monetary Fund: September 2013.

[10] **Key Indicators of the Labour Market (6th ed.).** International Labour Office: 2009. Also published online at www.ilo.org.

Latin America, Western Europe, and other developed regions over recent decades. Even in countries where women have traditionally been discouraged from working outside the home, their labor force numbers are rising. Except for a few nations that severely constrain women's roles, women's economic power — as labor and as consumer/decision-maker — is growing throughout the world.

Flatter Organizations

Another impact on the global workforce is the trend toward flatter organizations with decentralized decision-making and an emphasis on collaborative processes. I'll talk more about this in the context of U.S. organizations in the next section. Here I will just emphasize that, when evaluating global talent, the tiers are not as neatly drawn as they were in the past. Someone without an obvious title like "Vice President" or "Director" may still have significant experience with strategy, decision-making, supervision, and other responsibilities traditionally associated with positions in middle management or higher.

What's the takeaway here? All of these trends add up to the near-certainty of mid-sized and large companies in the U.S. needing to learn to manage individuals with a range of cultural backgrounds, workstyles, and expectations. Employees can't leave their upbringing, what they value, and who they are at the doorstep when they enter the workplace. Rather, the workplace must evolve from a traditional "one-size-fits-all" schema toward a paradigm where programs, policies, and management approaches transform to fit different individuals and groups. Issues like work/life balance, flex time, parenting/caregiving, communication style, lines of leadership and authority, and so on are the beginning, not the end, of that evolution.

This isn't just about changing a few policies. The human element — starting with senior leadership and managers — is absolutely essential. Rather than expecting everyone to assimilate to the corporate culture, we have entered an age where the best results will come from corporate leaders capable of what I call "reverse acculturation." The most successful leaders will be those who develop a global presence of mind, exercise cultural sensitivity, and inspire people from diverse cultures not to "assimilate" but to *contribute* their unique qualities to a dynamically growing corporate culture.

U.S. Workforce Trends

For U.S. companies, national workforce trends are as profoundly impactful as those related to globalization. To state the obvious, the U.S. population has changed — and will continue to change — significantly. Its size (308.7 million as of the 2010 census) has more than doubled since 1950, and its diversity has expanded even more profoundly. This is driven by two forces that will continue altering the U.S. workforce well into the future: immigration and racial and ethnic diversification.

Immigration

Immigration has long been an important component of U.S. population growth, with the net immigration rate projected to be positive (in-migration exceeding out-migration) for the full century from 1950 to 2050. The rate of net migrants per 1,000 resident population has shown increases in recent decades, and the U.S. Census Bureau projects that net immigration will continue at higher rates. Average annual inflow of immigrants over the decades shows what this looks like in terms of people entering the workforce. In the 1950s, average annual inflow was 252,000 immigrants; by the 1990s, that jumped to more than 900,000. The number of legal immigrants in the past decade surpassed 1 million annually in 2001 and 2002, and was above 1.1 million for 2005 through 2009.[11] During the last three decades, new immigrants have been predominantly Hispanic and Asian, and in younger age groups with higher participation rates. As a result, it is projected that in 2050 Asians will have the highest participation rate in the labor force — 65% — followed closely by Hispanics, with 64%.[12]

---

[11] **Yearbook of Immigration Statistics, 2009**. U.S. Dept. of Homeland Security: 2010. Also available online at www.dhs.gov/files/statistics/publications/yearbook.shtm.

[12] Toossi, Mitra. "A century of change: the U.S. labor force, 1950–2050." *Monthly Labor Review*: May 2002.

Racial and Ethnic Diversification

Because major racial and ethnic groups are aging at different rates, depending upon fertility, mortality, and immigration, some groups are comprising larger and larger percentages of the civilian noninstitutional[13] population. Consider these projections between 2000 and 2050:

- White non-Hispanics are expected to slowly decrease, making up 54% of the civilian noninstitutional population by 2050. (The general population of white non-Hispanics is projected to decrease between 2040 and 2050.)
- The Hispanic population, which had a 5.2% growth rate from 1980–1990 and continued growing by more than 3% through 2010, is expected to make up 23% of the civilian noninstitutional population by 2050.
- The black population, expected to increase at a much lower rate in future decades than in the past, is projected to constitute 15% of the total population by 2050.
- The "Asian and other" category is projected to grow considerably in the years ahead, and make up 10% of the total civilian noninstitutional population in 2050.[14]

If we were to add a third demographic force to the list it would certainly be that the U.S. population is aging. Many companies are acutely aware of the impending "experience drain" that may happen as Baby Boomers begin exiting the workforce en masse. While economic factors are causing many Boomers to forego early retirement and extend their careers, the exodus is inevitable — as is the surge of the next sizable generation: the Millennials.

---

[13] As defined at www.businessdictionary.com: "People who live in the U.S., are older than 16, and are not in an institution (criminal, mental, or other types of facilities) or active duty military personnel. This population figure is used in many statistics, including the civilian unemployment rate."

[14] Toosi, Mitra. "A century of change: the U.S. labor force, 1950–2050." *Monthly Labor Review:* May 2002.

Turning away from demographics, let's return to the corporate trend I mentioned in the previous section: the flattening, or decentralization, of power structures. In conjunction with trends toward downsizing, creation of more specialty firms, and proliferation of smaller consultancies and independent contractors, what has resulted is a U.S. workforce where more people have at least some experience with strategic decision-making.

In itself, that's a good thing. But simply eliminating layers of middle management and pushing accountability and responsibility down through the firm's hierarchy isn't enough to ensure success — for either individuals or the corporation. Yes, on the surface, that flattens hierarchies and gives more people a chance to make decisions about, and take ownership of, the work they do. But thinking about what I call the "three-legged stool" of responsibility, accountability, and empowerment, unless an organization takes steps to empower workers in decision-making — including being visibly inclusive and supportive of diverse individuals and points of view — outcomes will be less than satisfactory for all involved.

In most cases where I've heard people complaining that decentralization isn't working, a lopsided stool — lacking its "empowerment" leg — is the culprit. This can be especially challenging with more diverse, multicultural workforces where managers may lack the confidence to truly push decision-making down through the ranks in the first place — and also have gaps in cultural understanding that prevent them from knowing how and when to offer needed support.

Nonetheless, this trend from hierarchical structures to flatter, matrix-based organizations highlights again the critical importance of human capital (HC) and, by extension, the need for mature HC functions and a comprehensive talent strategy. Simply put, talent has moved to the forefront in terms of competitive position.

* * * * *

Understanding the global and U.S. workforce trends we've just discussed is an important first step toward effectively managing talent and gaining a competitive edge amidst rapid and ongoing market changes. To become a high-performing company, it is essential to identify, develop, and retain key talent — but also to regularly assess and adapt workforce strategies to make sure they are aligned with both the realities of the workforce and strategic business goals.

How *is* your talent measuring up competitively? The Institute for Corporate Productivity (i4cp) suggests that high-performing companies typically measure two key metrics — not just the more obvious "quality of hire," but also "quality of movement," which includes internal place-ment rate (IPR), as well as the following:

- Promotion Rates
- Internal Movement Rate
- Retention (After IPR, Promotion, or other Move)
- Succession Plan Compliance/Leadership Health

Workplace balance, diversity, and equality are deeply entwined with achieving success in these respects. This is not a question of political correctness. It is a business opportunity, and in many indus-tries a competitive necessity. To assess how you're doing in these areas, ask yourself these questions:

- Are differences in backgrounds leading to increased conflict or miscommunication between different individuals or teams?
- Are customs, language or other practices being used in ways that effectively exclude some people from groups, discussions, or decision-making?
- Does the organization's diversity commitment seem to attach to "minority" groups only, while getting little traction or engagement from the mainstream culture?
- Do diverse team members seem exclusively involved with their own group rather than with the team and ultimately the organization as a whole?
- Are organizational networks inclusive, or does networking tend to only involve people with similar backgrounds?
- Are different cultural groups finding it difficult to cooperate on projects? Is there a lack of group cohesion? (Cohesion is sometimes taken for granted

when group members are similar, because existing commonalities form a basis to extend cohesion in new directions. With groups made up of different members, cohesion often requires a more conscious effort or leadership guidance.)

If you answered yes to one or more of those questions, you're not alone. But the situations described above all restrict performance — so don't settle for this as your status quo. Now is the time to begin taking proactive steps to get to the point where you can read each question above and honestly say, "No, that's not a problem at our organization anymore."

New Talent Power Centers

To attract, develop, and manage today's talent effectively, we must first ask where it comes from, what it looks like, how to motivate it, and so on. In the U.S., the answers to these questions are not the same today as they were 20 or 30 years ago. In fact, several new "talent power centers" have arisen that are critically important to understand and integrate into your talent strategy. Each talent center is composed of distinct subcultures in which individual members have their own work ethos, identity, and values. If encouraged and supported, these groups represent new sources of "talent power" in that their diverse cultural, experiential, and interpersonal contributions drive fresh insights, innovation, creativity, and ultimately competitive advantage.

Conversely, organizations constrained by a "one size fits all" talent management philosophy risk alienating talent from these groups. That can lead to team and individual underperformance — and the loss of some of your best talent to competitors who are more inclusive and invest in developing their full potential.

Whether these groups already make up a significant percentage of your existing workforce, or are currently a small fraction, they are all *growing*. Today's corporations cannot afford to ignore these emerging talent centers any more than they can afford to ignore emerging technologies or changing market demands.

The LGBT Talent Power Center

Lesbian, gay, bisexual, and transgender (LGBT) employees constitute a sizeable, dynamic workforce population and distinct subculture within any corporation. While this population is not "new," growing mainstream acceptance of LGBT individuals in the U.S. and many other areas of the world has led to increased identification *as* a distinct population, and rightful expectations of fair and equal treatment. Recognizing the breadth and contributions of this talent power center, high-performing companies have been quick to put appropriate policies in place, ensure a respectful work environment, and take measures to welcome and support LGBT employees throughout recruitment, development, and advancement into leadership.

There are multiple incentives for *all* businesses to follow the lead of high-performing organizations when it comes to sharpening their credentials as LGBT-inclusive employers. Beyond tapping the extraordinary potential of this talent base, there is the likelihood that, for most companies, LGBT individuals also represent an important segment of their *customer* base. With expendable net income estimated at $790 billion in 2012[15] and certain to continue growing, LGBT consumers are an enormous market — and one that will direct its expendable dollars toward companies that support their community and values. Additionally, there is a large, fast-growing community of LGBT "allies" who are not lesbian, gay, bisexual, or transgender, but care a great deal about whether the companies they work for and buy from are supportive and respectful of LGBT friends and family.

In the U.S., building a pro-LGBT culture and brand can include LGBT-focused job fairs, communicating inclusion to the community at large through advertising, and sponsoring annual Gay Pride events, LGBT film festivals, and other relevant activities. Many large organizations are now on board with efforts like this, and many have LGBT networks or programs. To become a high performer, however, it is

---

[15] "America's LGBT 2012 Buying Power Projected at $790 Billion." Published online at www.witeck.com/pressreleases/americas-lgbt-2012-buying-power-projected-at-790-billion/. Witeck Communications: 2012.

necessary to expand these discrete efforts into a more thoroughly integrated approach that connects the LGBT community, and the individual talent and leadership from that community, with the development and implementation of fundamental business strategies.

For corporations with global workplaces, there is sometimes a more complex balance to strike. Credibility depends upon upholding core LGBT policies and values for every employee, anywhere a company does business. At the same time, the cultural dynamics of different countries where the company operates should be kept in mind. Successful LGBT inclusion efforts must be based in an understanding of local legal frameworks, regional knowledge and customs, and the surrounding culture's beliefs and norms. This understanding will help leaders and implementers of LGBT initiatives to anticipate potential challenges and tailor the core policies and values to meet the unique needs of each locale.

Enhancing recruitment, inclusion, promotion, and retention of LGBT employees represents a critical business imperative. A talent strategy that does not pay close attention to this talent center is not only inadequate, it is ultimately a risk to corporate reputation and brand value.

Generational Synergy as a Talent Power Center

Because of their sheer numbers, and unique background as the world's first "digital natives," it is logical to identify Millennials (generally, those born between 1980 and 2000) as an emerging talent center. However, I'd like to expand this view. In my experience, the real "talent power" that high-performing organizations are able to tap involves harnessing the diverse and complementary strengths that span the unique range of generations that make up today's workforce.

You may question whether "generation" really needs to influence talent strategy at all. But reflect on this further and you will see that the generation we are born into, and develop with throughout our lives, often has just as much — or more — impact on us than other aspects of our background. Each generation shares a set of formative events and trends — from headlines and heroes to parenting styles, educational systems, sociopolitical norms, and more. While behaviors and social contexts change, and individuals learn new skills and ideas throughout their lives, these fundamental building blocks and perceptual frames often remain consistent. People from the same generation often "get" each other in ways that transcend other differences; likewise, even when people come from similar backgrounds and are in the same professional field, generational differences can still create significant challenges and misunderstandings.

What makes generation especially important right now is that the U.S. is experiencing a historically unique situation: *four* generations working side by side in many workplaces. 20-year-old new hires may well find themselves interacting with colleagues who are older than them by 50 years or more!

If we examine each of the generations, it quickly becomes evident that their differences present some daunting challenges — but also tremendous potential synergies — in terms of talent management. Those born before 1946 are referred to as the World War II Generation. Most still working today were children during the war, but it remains a centrally influential event in their lives. Next are the Baby Boomers — products of the post-World War II boom in births between 1946 and 1964. Much smaller in size, the generation born between 1965 and 1980 is referred to as Generation X. And then come the Millennials, another larger generation born between 1980 and 2000, for whom personal computers, Internet technology, and cell phones have always been "normal" parts of life — and work.

There are several factors contributing to this rich generational mix in the workforce that likely will maintain that mix for years to come. In particular, labor shortages and the economic recession that started in 2007 have convinced many of those from the World War II and Baby Boomer generations to forego retirement. Combined with changes in Social Security and other pensions and retirement benefits, as well as increased life expectancy and lifestyle changes and medical advances that have helped offset some of the effects of aging, the bottom line is that it is not unusual for people to be working, or planning to work, well into their 70s or even longer.

Members of the two elder generations are remaining in the workforce longer, but proportional dynamics continue to shift. For example, in 2006, Boomers held the majority of positions of power and influence in U.S. organizations, constituting about 44% of the workforce. By 2011, that had dropped to 38%, while the percentage of Millennials in the workforce burgeoned from 15% to 25% during the same period.[16]

It would be an understatement to say that this creates some very interesting workplace interactions. Baby Boomers with decades of institutional knowledge are trying to develop camaraderie with team members whose on-the-job experience amounts to a semester internship, but whose ease with technology they can't match. Members of Generation X are making decisions and crafting policies that impact colleagues old enough to be their grandparents — or young enough to be their children. World War II Generation employees may find themselves taking orders from a talented young manager who is from the same generation as their *great*-grandchildren.

Each of these generations has its own values, work styles, and expectations — and having team members from three or even four generations trying to navigate such differences while working on the same project team can create the conditions for a perfect storm, or what I refer to as the "Clash of Generations." But those same differences, if properly monitored, coached, and steered, can also drive collaborations that yield unprecedented success. This is why I recommend treating the generational mix itself, rather than any one generation, as a talent power center worthy of executive-level attention and development.

The Female Talent Power Center

In 2010, 58% of all undergraduate degrees in the U.S. were awarded to women. Women accounted for 53% of the total college-educated population, and 50% of college-educated workers. The total number of females in the labor force is also projected to be growing at a slightly faster rate than men — 7.4% compared to 6.3% from 2010 to

---

[16] Labor Force Projections tables, Civilian Labor Force 2004-2014. Published online at www.bls.gov/emp/emplab1.htm. Bureau of Labor Statistics: 2013.

2020. Women make up almost half of all U.S. workers (49.9%), 51% of people in professional careers, and *more than two-thirds* of employees in ten of the 15 job categories expected to grow the fastest in the next few years, including healthcare sector jobs such as personal care aides and physical therapists.[17]

Statistics also show that women have become a driving factor in the success of the U.S. economy since the 1970s. Indeed, the additional productive power of women entering the workforce from 1970 until today accounts for about a quarter of the current GDP.[18]

Few would disagree that women represent a critical talent power center for today's corporations. Many executives would no doubt say women are *the* talent center they consider most important to long-term success, and quite a few companies have invested in initiatives, programs, training, leadership development, and other resources specifically aimed at women. There is wide recognition that, at a Macro level, we can continue raising female labor participation rates, and, within corporations, where many high-skill women are employed, there is rich potential to advance more women into leadership positions and benefit from the unique skills and contributions they offer.

Unfortunately, that potential — not to mention the rising aspirations of individual women — is a long way from being fulfilled. Despite the sincere efforts of major corporations, the proportion of women falls quickly as we look higher in the corporate hierarchy. This picture has not improved for years. Women have been encouraged to climb the occupational ladder only to discover that men dominate the middle rungs and the upper rungs are out of reach. Only 2% of Fortune 500 CEOs, five CEOs in the FTSE 100, and less than 13% of U.S. board

---

[17] **Occupational Outlook Handbook, 2012-13 Edition, Projections Overview**. Published online at www.bls.gov/ooh/about/projections-overview.htm. Bureau of Labor Statistics, U.S. Department of Labor: 2014.

[18] Barsch, Joanna; Lareina Yee. "Unlocking the Full Potential of Women in the U.S. Economy." McKinsey & Company: April 2011. Available online at www.mckinsey.com/client_service/organization/latest_thinking/unlocking_the _full_potential.

members are women.[19] Men dominate the upper ranks of management consultancies and banks.

On the positive side, women in the U.S. have demonstrated what they can do by successfully running some of the world's top brands, including PepsiCo, Xerox, HP, and Yahoo. So — what more can your business do to better realize the full potential of this talent power center? As with all the talent power centers, an important first step is to try to understand the specific variables impacting members of this group, as well as their values, motivations, communication styles, and so on.

For example, while there is much to be said for rolling out a robust women's leadership development initiative, it is equally important to address practical issues like child care. In 2010, 64.2% of women with children younger than age 6, 61.1% of mothers with children younger than age 3, and 56.5% of mothers with children under a year old were in the labor force.[20] Clearly, more women are going back to work sooner after giving birth, but this can create tremendous strain in terms of child care, particularly for single moms. Understandably, access to employer-provided child-care arrangements has been shown to lead to greater job stability and retention for such women. With an aging workforce and a more skill-dependent economy in the U.S., practical measures like this are essential to enable female talent to contribute what corporations need them to contribute.

Similarly, to make substantial progress in developing and advancing women on the path to leadership, companies must go beyond setting goals and talking the talk. To be effective, efforts must genuinely engage women and address the specific challenges they face. A few top-level recommendations in this regard:

- Institutionalize structural changes through executive sponsorships to aid the development of female leaders

---

[19] "Women in Senior Management: Still Not Enough." *Grant Thornton International Business Report, 2012.* Grant Thornton International Ltd.: 2012.

[20] **Women in the labor force: A databook (2010 edition).** Published online at www.bls.gov/cps/wlf-databook-2011.pdf. Bureau of Labor Statistics, U.S. Department of Labor: 2011.

- Create a robust mentoring program that matches men and women at different leadership levels
- Assess and refine your integrated talent management and total rewards strategy in the context of what it takes to hire, develop, and retain women specifically
- Challenge status quo cultural perceptions, stereotypes, and corporate customs that impede women from advancing up the career ladder
- Blend hands-on development opportunities with advanced learning and training
- Provide support mechanisms such as day care, options for care-giving, etc.
- Look for opportunities to integrate women's interests with broader workforce interests; instead of a "women only" approach to flex-time, for example, create a flex-time policy that benefits everyone

The Asian Talent Power Center

The percentage of Asians in the U.S. has increased dramatically, from just 1% in 1965 to 6.2% by 2011.[21] Among the 33.5 million foreign-born individuals (11.7% of the U.S. population), 25% were born in Asia. These numbers are expected to continue to grow rapidly. In some regions of the country, such as the mid-Atlantic states, the Asian population has grown by 60% over the past decade. Four out of 10 Asian Americans live on the West Coast, but the Washington, D.C. area has also become a noteworthy Asian hub, including the nation's fourth-highest concentration of Asian Indians and Koreans.[22]

What makes Asian Americans a vital talent power center is not just the raw numbers, but also the fact that, by and large, they are one of

---

[21] Munroe, Tapan. "Contribution of Asians to the Economy." Published online at http://tmunroe.wordpress.com/2012/07/02/contribution-of-asian-americans-to-the-economy/. July 2, 2012.

[22] Morello, Carol, and Dan Keating. "D.C. region's Asian population is up 60 percent since 2000, census data show." *The Washington Post:* May 26, 2011.

the most educationally prepared groups in the labor force. Asian cultures tend to urge attainment of higher education as a path to both individual and professional success. As a result, Asian expertise and entrepreneurial spirit have been quite evident as economic drivers in the U.S., particularly in high-tech and knowledge-based industries, and in world-class innovation hubs like the Silicon Valley, where they account for roughly a third of the scientific and engineering workforce. During the late 1980s and 1990s, approximately a quarter of Silicon Valley high-tech firms had Indian or Chinese CEOs.[23]

Unfortunately, that's the exception; most Asians plateau without reaching the C-suite. Too often, organizations have constrained this talent center to largely technical areas, with minimal access to higher levels of decision-making. There is disproportionate underrepresentation of Asians in high-level administration in general, with many talented individuals stagnating on lower levels of the managerial ladder.

What can corporations do to better utilize this highly educated subculture and unleash their entrepreneurial spirit, innovation, and creativity? First, executives should take a hard look at whether there is an inherent bias against moving Asians, particularly those from other countries, into top leadership positions. Sometimes a de facto "All-American" leadership network exists — and, although perhaps not intentionally, that network may put up barriers to those with different accents or birthplaces. Consciously addressing this potential bias and removing any barriers is critical.

It is also important to recognize aspects of Asian culture that may undermine an individual's ability to ascend through the ranks of a U.S. corporate culture. For example, Asian cultures are generally more communitarian and highly respectful of authority, so individuals may be less inclined to assert themselves, promote their achievements, or challenge decisions — qualities that tend to be important to advancing in a U.S. organization. As you're grooming Asian talent, a key part of coaching and mentoring, then, is to help individuals understand that

[23] Saxenian, AnnaLee. **Silicon Valley's New Immigrant Entrepreneurs**. Public Policy Institute of California. San Francisco, CA: 1999.

challenging and asserting are good traits and will not be viewed as "too aggressive" or disrespectful.

Other suggestions for improving success with the Asian talent center are talent strategy best practices in general. Companies should evaluate policies in terms of how well they ensure inclusivity, for example. Promotion opportunities, particularly appointments to management and senior leadership, should be coordinated and planned in order to offset any artificial barriers which stem from cultural stereotypes. Formal channels should be institutionalized to encourage participation in projects that provide on-the-job training and preparation for future assignments, including those leading to management. Opportunities should be provided for employees to utilize and develop both existing and latent skills in present job assignments as well as roles they aspire to or would simply like to learn about.

Of course, one of the most important ways to ensure success with Asians — and across your entire multicultural workforce — is to make interest, sensitivity, competence, and experience in working with a diverse labor force key criteria for rewards and promotions into management, particularly senior-level appointments.

The Hispanic/Latino Talent Power Center

The rapid growth of the U.S. Hispanic and Latino population has not only prompted more and more companies to hire individuals from this talent power center, but has also moved them to seek out managers and employees who understand the language and culture. According to *Hispanic Business Week*, 41.3 million Hispanics now comprise 14% of the U.S. population and are its fastest growing segment.[24] The U.S. Census Bureau projects that this group will constitute 24% of the nation's population by 2050.[25] From a workforce perspective, it is also significant

---

[24] Gangemi, Jeffrey. "Demand for Hispanic MBAs Is Caliente." Published online at www.businessweek.com/stories/2005-12-03/demand-for-hispanic-mbas-is-caliente. *BloombergBusinessweek*: December 3, 2005.

[25] Vincent, Grayson K., and Victoria A. Velkoff. **The Next Four Decades — The Older Population in the United States: 2010-2050**. U.S. Department of Commerce Economics and Statistics Administration, U.S. Census Bureau: 2010.

that Hispanics are the youngest segment of the U.S. workforce, with 50% under age 35.[26] According to the Pew Hispanic Center, they are the most likely of all racial or ethnic groups to seek work and will account for half of labor growth through 2020.[27]

In short, it is indisputable that Hispanics and Latinos are a critical component of our next generation of workers — and that recruiting and leveraging this talent will be essential for future business success.

Given that, companies must develop proactive strategies to attract and develop this key workforce segment. Again, one size does not fit all — Hispanic and Latino workforce development needs are different from other groups because their cultural experiences are different. Keeping this group's deep cultural roots in mind when developing your talent strategy will ensure that it is effective. For example, with Hispanics and Latinos, it is especially important to:

- Build trust and relationships by demonstrating empathy and moral support
- Be mindful of the social and familial responsibilities this group tends to have; work/life balance, flex time, and respect for their family obligations are all vital in helping them commute between their cultural and work roles
- Provide a supportive environment to help them address professional and personal challenges, including programs to enhance confidence and self-esteem, and coaching/mentoring to deal with possible promotional anxieties
- Equip them with the tools and training they need to perform their jobs effectively, which may include being sensitive to language needs

[26] "State of the Hispanic Consumer: The Hispanic Market Imperative." Published online at www.nielsen.com/us/en/reports/2012/state-of-the-hispanic-consumer-the-hispanic-market-imperative.html. The Nielson Company: 2012.

[27] "Hispanics: A People in Motion." Chapter in **Trends 2005**. Pew Research Center: 2005.

- Watch for possible conflict avoidance and use sensitivity in teaching or facilitating paths to resolution; "saving face" is very important
- Allow for self-reflection in the context of their distinct culture and professional performance

Hispanics and Latinos tend to have a strong sense of destiny as part of their worldview, along with a high degree of acceptance of hierarchy and status, both at work and in familial or social settings. Acceptance of power distance, including respect toward elders and superiors, influences their work interactions. Promoting team relation-ships can channel these qualities as strengths. At the same time, assertiveness, decision-making, and being willing to challenge authority may not come naturally and may need to be coached and encouraged. All of this must be taken into consideration in order to successfully leverage the potential of this talent center.

Globalizing Your Talent Strategy

As the statistics in this chapter make clear, there is no way around the fact that the U.S. workforce is becoming increasingly diverse. That's partly from demographic trends, and partly from an economic evolution that has both employees and employers migrating more easily to different parts of the world.

Does this global talent pool present challenges? Of course. We can't just throw people from different cultural backgrounds into the same workplace and expect everything to go without a hitch. That's equally true when it comes to different cultural dispositions among those from the same country, including those tied to race, ethnicity, sexual orientation, religion, age, disability, and so on.

The social tensions engendered by this increasing diversity are real, as are the risks of related workplace conflict, miscommunication, and other difficulties. Such tensions may also get amplified in the short term by broader economic or political failures. But the opportunities here are just as real. If managed well, a multicultural workforce can ex-pand and strengthen your corporate culture, deliver new innovations due to the broader range of perspectives, and tap new synergies that drive higher overall performance.

Minimizing the risks, and maximizing the benefits, of a diverse, global workforce really depends on how well an organization adapts, including evolving hierarchical structures into more self-managed work teams, bringing in needed expertise (either through internal hiring and development or via external consultants), and putting policies and programs in place to ensure inclusivity, fairness, and effective advancement of employees who may have very different development needs. Over all of this, there is the need for senior executives to globalize their perspective, develop multicultural leadership skills, and shift talent development and other key business strategies to reflect the new realities of a global workforce and marketplace. We'll talk more about these adaptations in the next chapter.

The payoffs of doing this work are significant. Understanding cultural differences doesn't just make it easier to manage an increasingly diverse, multicultural workforce, it also gives U.S. companies one of the essential tools to succeed in expanding operations and markets beyond our borders.

In one sense, the talent equation is very straightforward. Talent, or human capital, has become the primary value driver in many industries, and is directly related to the quality of a company's products, services, technology, customer relations, and innovation. The best and brightest talent now comes from all over the world, and with a wide range of needs and values. Business success therefore depends on having a talent strategy, and management at all levels that can attract, develop, and retain global talent better than your competitors.

As the economy bounces back, those who don't feel engaged or respected by their current employer will be quicker than ever to seek new opportunities. Those losing these employees face the high cost of increased recruiting and training for replacements. Those gaining these employees not only get the immediate payoff of their experience and skill, they also gain momentum as an attractive "talent brand."

Remember, in today's world, top talent can go anywhere. To get them to your company, and keep them for years, your company must have a reputation for investing in, developing, rewarding, and promoting talent. In a diverse, global environment, your company must also make appropriate emotional connections with, and have an authentic employer value proposition that appeals to, employees with different backgrounds. Perhaps more than any other factor, I believe this is what will distinguish tomorrow's corporate high performers from the rest of the pack.

CHAPTER 2

Agility and a Global Mindset
in the Executive Suite

In today's talent environment, productivity, innovation, and other competitive drivers depend on the groups comprising the diverse, global workforce all feeling accepted, respected and included. High-performing companies get this, and have established accepting cultures where team members from diverse groups are visibly succeeding in all areas, and at all levels of decision-making. On the opposite end of the spectrum, some organizations exhibit little or no acceptance toward employees from different backgrounds, and prevailing attitudes and practices actively undermine the kind of inclusivity that increasingly will be required for businesses to succeed.

I use the word "inclusivity" very purposefully, for, as I will discuss further in Chapter 4, this goes beyond simply diversifying the workforce. Demographics, market realities, and legal regulations already cause more companies to hire a wider range of people when it comes to race, ethnicity, national origin, sexual orientation, disabilities, and so on. Unfortunately, after being hired, many of these people experience stereotyping and discrimination, overt and covert, that *excludes* them from the overall culture and prevents them from contributing their full value.

Inclusivity, by contrast, means inviting and embracing people's differences — and proactively *including* differences as a normal part of interactions, practices, and the corporate culture in general. It means encouraging inclusive *behavior* throughout the organization. That doesn't stop with welcoming individual ideas or dissenting opinions on business decisions — it also extends to cultural and social mores.

The transition from stereotyping and other ingrained forms of exclusivity to an inclusive workplace is not easy. Stereotyping is tied to a natural human tendency to "categorize" as part of mentally organizing and making sense of the world. Because our categories typically rely on surface-level differences and assumptions rather than deeper experience or understanding, they often "misframe" or distort our perception of others, including their talents, motivations, and potential contributions in work settings.

Still, we can't expect people to instantly drop stereotypes they've held for decades just because the workforce has become more diverse and a "celebrate diversity" plank has been added to the company's core values. The reality is that true inclusivity will only happen if there is strong executive leadership in this area. Leaders drive the workplace culture — especially when it comes to change. As an executive, you set your company's behavioral standards through your words and actions as much as through policies and procedures. It is critical to "walk the walk" in resisting the urge to stereotype and making it clear that excluding those who are different is unacceptable.

In addition to leading by example, it is also important to actively educate and coach others on the value of inclusive behavior, starting with peers on the leadership team. But if you stop at the senior leadership level, you will not transform the culture. Always remember that, especially in large organizations, front-line employees tend to take their cues from the manager they interact with regularly.

When communicating why everyone in the organization should adopt a more inclusive mindset, humanistic reasons are certainly important, but don't ignore the practical business motives. Stereotyping negatively affects morale and productivity. It hinders communication and teamwork and creates "us vs. them" thinking where "in-groups" and "out-groups" guard information and behave in ways that serve their group's power rather than the best interests of the project, department, or company. Failing to include diverse employee perspectives and skills — or, worse, losing such employees to competitors — also constrains overall creativity, problem-solving, and competitive position. Reverberations can negatively impact many other areas: quality, process efficiency, customer service and more.

Conversely, treating inclusivity as a strategic imperative is becoming one of the variables that separates high performers from mediocre and underperforming businesses. In that context, let's start this chapter by looking at "three pillars" of competitive advantage that belong at the forefront of every discussion on diversity: human capital, costs and productivity, and innovation.

Maximize the Value of Human Capital

As I will emphasize throughout this book, human capital has become a primary (if not *the* primary) competitive differentiator in most industries. It is essential to attract, develop, and retain the most qualified, "best fit" talent. At the same time, scarcity of top-tier talent in many fields, increased mobility, and the infinite search power of the Internet enable top candidates to be very selective in choosing where to work. In short, to get top-tier employees, you have to prove that you are a top-tier *employer*!

This makes ***employer brand management*** critical. Leaders should constantly evaluate how effectively the corporate culture, benefits, and opportunities for advancement create an employer brand that appeals to high-performing talent. Within the talent acquisition phase, that includes assessing, improving, and delivering on an authentic ***employer value proposition*** as well as being a brand ambassador who champions the organization as a great place to work.

But it would be a huge mistake to think that employer brand management ends there. On the contrary, once the talent is in, executives must continue to reinforce the employer value proposition in their roles as coach, talent development architect, and the most visible "face" or "voice" of the organization. And, with a diverse, global workforce, inclusivity *must* be part of the value proposition that you deliver every day.

The importance of this cannot be overstated. In today's market, it is very easy for talent to constantly compare (and seize!) external opportunities. Loyalty isn't granted at the moment of hire — it must be continually earned (and deepened) by tangible experience of what makes the organization an exceptional employer. Inclusivity is a necessary part of that. If people feel excluded, they may jump to a more inclusive competitor even if you offer slightly better pay and benefits.

Across many segments of the workforce, "WIIFM" (What's In It For Me?) is an increasingly vital criterion. Since the answers will vary greatly in a diverse workforce, being a top employer brand may depend less on superiority in one area than on evidence of your ongoing commitment, and flexibility, in giving individual employees what they want across a wide range of possibilities.

Reduce Costs, Improve Productivity

Everyone "gets" this second pillar of competitive advantage on the fundamental level. Most organizations also track a range of workforce cost and productivity measures. However, in my experience, bottom-line impacts related to the workforce are often underestimated. And, more to the point of our discussion in this book, the impact of managing (or failing to manage) the challenges presented by today's more diverse workforce is frequently overlooked.

Employee turnover is a prime example. A workplace where diversity is not respected and little effort is made to bridge differences between cultures and subcultures will inevitably see higher turnover. Conversely, taking steps to create an inclusive, high-satisfaction, low-turnover workplace delivers savings in obvious areas like recruitment and training, and even more value in "ripple effect" improvements. In almost any area of any business, greater efficiency and quality will be a natural outcome of team members staying together long enough to develop authentic, respectful relationships, discover complementary strengths, and bond over both individual and team accomplishments.

Similarly, the better you cover your bases when it comes to workplace diversity and inclusion, the more you will reduce the risks, costs, and brand damage associated with grievances, complaints, and lawsuits related to issues like discrimination and sexual harassment. But a genuinely welcoming workplace that is satisfying for all employees has bottom-line benefits well beyond that! Improvements in morale and reduction of job-related stress consistently boost productivity, lower absenteeism, and drive better performance across the board.

Drive Innovation

Most organizations embrace the value of innovation, and many have whole business units dedicated to it. The role of workplace diversity in *driving* innovative, breakthrough thinking and solutions,

54

however, is rarely given enough attention. The think about the broad definitions of "diversity" and "inclusion" and you will see that these principles are absolutely vital to innovation and creativity. The capacity to generate new, "outside-the-box" ideas and insights truly *depends* on having multiple voices from multiple backgrounds and perspectives who feel invited to embrace and express *differences*. That's "diversity and inclusion"!

The business case for investing in workforce diversity and inclusion is therefore intrinsically linked to a company's innovation strategy. Are you looking to the power of innovation to help drive operational excellence? Or increase market penetration? Or expand into new markets? Or differentiate your brand? A diverse workforce, empowered by an inclusive culture, gives you the "innovative fuel" to achieve these goals. Yes, it also presents challenges, and you must find ways to channel the multiplicity of views in ways that serve strategic objectives. However, innovation *without* diversity and inclusion is like a high-performance sports car with an empty gas tank.

These "three pillars" I've discussed are not revolutionary — almost every executive sees talent, cost/productivity, and innovation as fundamental to their organization's success. By emphasizing them in *my* work, I'm trying to underline the point that diversity and inclusion should not be treated as separate from other business practices. On the contrary, I argue that, given the realities of today's business environment, diversity and inclusion should be an integral aspect of everything from top-level strategy down to basic business processes. When they are not, tremendous opportunities to strengthen the three pillars are lost — and the pillars may even begin to crumble.

Establishing the "why" of focusing more attention on diversity and inclusion is a necessary first step. But let's move on to the "how." To start, I will spend the rest of this chapter on two general attributes that distinguish the executives who are most successful in managing today's multicultural workforce: agility and a global mindset.

Leading a Changing Workforce Demands Agility

Agility has become a hot topic in the business leadership community — for good reason. You can't excel as a leader in today's constantly evolving, global economy if you aren't flexible enough to adapt to change. That includes learning to skillfully lead an increasingly diverse workforce comprised of many individuals who are different from you in significant ways.

To be sure, traditional core competencies of leadership remain central to success, including articulating vision, inspiring and motivating subordinates, and maintaining integrity in relationships. What has changed, however, is that achieving these competencies requires a range of approaches with people from different backgrounds. For example, what motivates talent from Asian cultures will not be the same as what motivates talent from the U.S. Even looking just at the U.S.-born workforce, what motivates Millennials is different from what motivates Baby Boomers, there are motivational differences between men and women, and across many other groups.

In short, increased workforce diversity compels leaders to grapple with a host of new challenges, be aware of a wider range of issues, and be much more agile in their thinking, behavior, and management styles. What constituted good leadership just a generation ago will now fall short of the mark.

One area where today's leaders must have agility involves a fundamental shift in how "diversity" itself is approached. A generation ago, this was predominantly a compliance issue, and, to some degree, a humanistic one. Today, leaders in organizations that value (or aspire to value) diversity must be able to articulate the *business case* for diversity.

Effective leaders communicate (and indeed embody) an organizational vision that inspires and unites people throughout the organization. With a diverse workforce, that vision must incorporate an explicit understanding and promotion of the real value diversity adds to the organization.

In their classic article, "Managing Cultural Diversity: Implications for Organizational Competitiveness", Cox and Blake outlined several domains in which competitive advantage should derive from explicitly valuing diversity in an organization. Although their article was written in the early 1990s, these domains continue to be a fundamental starting point in presenting why diversity should be a strategic imperative rather than merely a question of compliance. The competitive advantages of diversity that they identified include the following:

- Enhanced skill in entering untapped markets
- Innovation and creativity flowing from new perspectives
- Increased ability to adapt to changing environments[28]

Building on these domains, I would note that diversity isn't just an advantage in the idea generation phase of innovation. We are increasingly seeing that it improves innovation *management* — that is, bringing new ideas successfully to fruition. Similarly, in thinking about the "ability to adapt to changing environments," it is worth emphasizing that a diverse, global workforce has become a tremendous asset in being able to adapt quickly and effectively to the almost endless range of business shifts that occur in today's highly globalized (and Internet-paced) business environment.

I would also add a new domain that has become vitally important as more companies do business in international markets: expanded, enhanced brand image with greater appeal for both local and global commerce. Conversely, having a brand that is perceived as lacking diversity and inclusiveness has become a serious competitive weakness.

In addition to their role in understanding and engineering competitive position, we expect leaders to be innovative thinkers with a deep sense of purpose. Where agility comes into play in this arena is that today's most successful leaders are not self-contained icons, they are people who actively reach out and engage *diverse* stakeholders, influencing and learning from them at the same time. They generate novel strategic insights, and effective operational approaches, by examining situations from multiple perspectives and being able to "connect the dots" between sometimes seemingly disparate issues or groups.

---

[28] Cox Jr., T.H., and S. Blake. "Managing Cultural Diversity: Implications for Organizational Competitiveness." *Academy of Management Executives 5:* 1991.

Because they are genuinely connecting *to* diverse stakeholders, they are able to create and present goals and programs that will resonate *for* diverse stakeholders.

Likewise, agile leaders develop a broad repertoire of communication tactics and behaviors that allow them to rapidly adjust their leadership style to the different individuals and circumstances involved in any given situation. They adopt the practice of always seeking feedback from multiple sources and using both mistakes and successes to drive continual learning and development. They exhibit sensitivity and resilience in responding to the difficulty and discomfort that change and uncertainty can bring — including those that arise from cultural differences. For themselves as well as those they lead, they also have the flexibility necessary to balance short-term demands with long-term priorities, top-down direction-setting with meaningful subordinate participation, and individual initiative with strong teamwork.

The culmination of an agile leader's efforts, and indeed the measure of their success, is that management, project teams, and the organization itself all display greater agility — and individuals throughout the organization become agile and effective leaders themselves. Of course, the benefits here are not limited to the realm of diversity — we are really talking about a key aspect of becoming a high-performing organization.

Indeed, a survey on Organizational and Leadership Agility conducted by i4cp in 2010 sought to identify the most important elements of organizational and leadership agility specifically in relation to high performance. Among many interesting findings, the survey asked the extent to which executive leadership culture posed *challenges* to increasing organizational agility. Survey respondents provided some excellent insights on how *not* to lead the way:

- 49.7% said their companies had mixed messages about the desirability of candid conversation and feedback
- 46.2% said executives were overly focused on their own "silos"
- 34.7% said agile leadership was not consistently modeled by top executives

- 34.4% said top executives did not sufficiently empower other management levels
- 30% said innovative thinking was not sufficiently encouraged or rewarded
- 29.9% of respondents said there was insufficient scanning for new trends and opportunities in the organizational environment[29]

The bottom line? To deal with the added complexities of globalization and a diversified workforce, companies must remove such obstacles and invest in leadership and organizational agility. Leaders like you are truly at the helm in navigating that change.

Global Business Demands a Global Mindset

In a global business competing in global markets with a global workforce, it is absolutely essential that executives embrace and model a "global mindset". This does not just mean adopting a more positive attitude about other countries. I am talking about a whole set of attitudes, values, behaviors, and skills that revolve around understanding, appreciating, and collaborating across cultures. In a sense, a global mindset is both a logical extension of, and the foundation for, the leadership and organizational agility we discussed in the previous section. It is a frame of mind that greatly expands the capacity to manage strategic complexity — and to not only survive but thrive in new and unknown situations.

Paraphrasing Stephen Rhinesmith, one of the world's leading experts on global leadership, a global mindset encourages the use of "global knowledge" in designing and executing strategies. This does not merely entail the sum of organizational capabilities, such as diverse linguistic abilities, cultural sensitivity training, global IT infrastructure,

---

[29] *Organizational and Leadership Agility Survey.* Also available online at www.i4cp.com/productivity-blog/2010/03/11/agile-leaders-generate-greater-corporate-performance. Institute for Corporate Productivity, Inc.: 2010.

and so on. We are talking about something more fundamental — a global way of thinking that influences everything from top-level strategy down to day-to-day interactions. Thinking globally changes how organizations and leaders approach organizational capabilities, assess threats and opportunities, and manage diverse talent. And only when this global mindset is pervasive will a company truly tap the potential of the most critical asset in becoming a high performer: its people.[30]

There have always been a few people with a global mindset of course. These are the people who are interested in exploring beyond their national borders and eager to engage in new experiences that stretch their knowledge and sense of purpose. In the corporate world, until very recently, this applied to the relative few managers and executives who rose to the challenges of early global business opportunities, and a small number of expatriates who used specialized skills to travel or permanently resettle in new countries.

Now, however, changes in technology, finance, political systems, business models, air travel and media have greatly expanded the number of people essentially operating in a global reality. In many business environments, international experience has become a prerequisite for a successful career. With more companies expanding operations and markets into multiple countries, even mid-level managers often find themselves working in new situations involving employees, vendors, clients and customers from multiple countries and cultures.

Whether from expanding overseas operations or a more diverse, multinational workforce here at home, the reality of "going global" is inevitably adding greater complexity in managerial roles: cross-border transactions, international regulations, cultural variations among workers, and much more. To manage this complexity successfully, it is imperative to understand the "foreign" environment and react in a timely and judicious manner in both business and people decisions.

Unfortunately, that kind of understanding — which really starts with adopting a global mindset — eludes a significant percentage of

---

[30] Rhinesmith, Stephen H. "Global Mindsets for Global Managers." *Training & Development,* October 1992.

those now deeply immersed in a global reality. As a result, a high number of people, including those at the highest levels of leadership, find themselves in confusing, frustrating situations — many of which have undesirable business impacts or outcomes. Indeed, one reason that executives reach out to a consulting firm like mine is to get a handle on what they need to do differently to better navigate the global reality that is rapidly expanding in every direction they turn.

But let's take a step back now. Before we talk about what it takes to develop and apply a global mindset, let's look at six common "challenges" for those with traditional mindsets that can become "opportunities" with a global mindset.

Global Interdependency

Global interdependency among companies has increased as a result of offshoring of business operations, migration of skilled workers across borders (particularly into the U.S.), and ever-widening supply chains and markets around the globe. More and more companies are connected with each other. In the traditional mindset, this complicates the flow of cross-border goods, money, and decisions and creates a plethora of new risks and challenges.

Leaders with a global mindset, however, are adept at exploring and deriving great value from cross-border business opportunities. In large part this depends on what I call "reverse acculturation." I touched on this concept in Chapter 1, and it will figure prominently throughout this book. Reverse acculturation is the opposite of assimilation. Rather than expecting other cultures to play by your rules, and becoming frustrated when they don't, reverse acculturation is taking the stance that it is your responsibility to understand the cultures of countries where your business operations exist and adapting operations to fit *their* environments. Another way to look at this is that, instead of demanding that local culture shrink to fit the existing corporate culture, you look at how the corporate culture can expand to *include* the local culture — with all its differences, and its natural strengths, intact. Companies that do this successfully tap the power of cross-cultural synergies that, under the traditional mindset, would more likely result in conflict.

Diversity

Diversity itself, especially when it includes multiple nations and cultures, can feel like a source of never-ending obstacles for someone with a "unicultural" mindset. Worse, the resulting myopic view can lead companies to constrain their own growth, limiting themselves to the confines of what they know rather than figuring out how to connect with the new value represented by diverse talent and customers.

Yes, cross-cultural or even simply cross-generational teams create challenges and require agile leadership to succeed. It can be tempting to see relying on homogeneous teams as the easier approach. However, teams made up of people from different disciplines, backgrounds, and cultures also frequently prove better able to achieve high performance, generate innovative ideas and execute breakthrough approaches.

But, in a sense, there's an even more basic argument for adopting a global mindset and welcoming diversity: It's not going to go away. Organizations will inevitably become more multinational (in many cases, they will have to in order to remain competitive), and workers from a wider range of cultures and subcultures will continue to expand the U.S. workforce. It's important to emphasize that diversity manifests not only through the workforce but also, increasingly, in every area of business: customers, vendors, suppliers, investors. The evolution of media and technology has brought the reality of diversity even to relatively small organizations that aren't actively globalizing operations.

In short, the choice is not whether you will have to deal with diversity — you will. The choice is whether to take the necessary steps to align strategies and how managers and employees approach diversity so that the end result is a dynamic work environment and higher performance rather than conflict and frustration. Leaders with a global mindset embrace this work — and are strengthening operations, talent, and competitive position as a result.

Constant Change

Rapid, unpredictable change in multiple areas and dimensions has become the norm in corporate environments. In many cases, the very configuration of the organization is also continuously shifting as companies evolve toward flatter hierarchies, engage in M&A activities, restructure in response to market changes or competitive pressures, and so on. Combine that with the emerging talent power centers in today's workforce, and you have a situation that can be very disturbing for those holding tightly to the frameworks and expectations of a past era. Not only are decision-making processes pushing lower into the corporate hierarchy, the decisions themselves are being made by different types of people. In some cases, these people may even be from, or located in, countries and cultures where concepts of authority or decision-making criteria do not match those of western executives (as we'll explore more fully in the next chapter).

This can become overwhelming for leaders who believe they must "save" an outdated status quo where "order" or "security" look and feel exactly like they did decades ago. But those who have a global mindset embrace these changes fully — and then manage them to maximum benefit. By putting time into understanding the new decision-makers throughout their workforce, they gain confidence in their people's capabilities at every level, with no misplaced fears based on stereotypes. Receptive to new possibilities and nimble in their leadership approach, they find ways to empower and motivate diverse talent, unleashing new sources of value and innovation. Unlike their more traditional peers, leaders with a global mindset do not see constant change as a "problem" — in fact, they see it as a reliable pipeline of opportunities to improve operations and sharpen their competitive edge.

Uncertainty

Globalization, combined with extraordinary technological developments, have created a conundrum for today's business leaders: more and more information is delivered, from more sources, with incredible speed, and yet there is often less and less clarity on how to transform all this data into insight and action. Cause-effect relationships have become blurred, making it difficult in some cases to even define clear, consistent value drivers. Image? Price? Related services? Innovation? Privileged relationships? Speed? Knowledge? Something else? Business processes, planning routines and systems that were once considered stable, permanent elements of the work environment have sometimes lost credibility and needed to be discarded or radically changed to keep up with a pace, breadth, and depth of change over the past few years that exceeds anything previously experienced. In short, today's executives are coping with high levels of uncertainty, ambiguity, and turbulence. Disruption has become almost commonplace.

Without diminishing the many profound uncertainties generated directly or indirectly by the global financial crisis, it is unlikely that it's just a matter of time until organizations can return to a "pre-crisis" stability. Too much has changed, and continues to change — both in the technological sphere and due to our increasingly complex, interconnected global economic and social reality. I believe uncertainty must be accepted as a real and constantly present aspect of business. That necessitates new approaches and capabilities — some of which may not be apparent now, yet become mission-critical in a matter of months.

Here again, leaders with a global mindset have a distinct advantage. Because of their natural inclination to see new developments as potential opportunities for improvement, innovation, and growth, they are constantly scanning the internal and external business environments. This allows them to be more proactive in managing emerging areas of uncertainty — whether it's something as simple as providing additional reassurance and guidance to the workforce, or as complex as getting ahead of the curve in meeting new market needs. Leaders with a traditional mindset are too often stuck in a more reactionary mode. They may fail to "see" (or consciously avoid looking at) aspects of the business environment that challenge or conflict with their thinking and perspectives. Certainly, I have seen this in some cases with regard to diverse, global talent. Instead of proactively embracing this reality and making changes that would deliver ongoing benefits, some executives ignore the trends and demographics until reality literally forces them to react. At that point, they're no longer able to strategically manage and gain competitive advantage; they are instead in pure damage control mode.

Subcultures

One test of the global mindset — and even globally oriented people come up short on this at times — is how well a leader understands "differences within a difference." A working understanding of another country or a workforce group different from your own is the *beginning*

64

of the journey, not the end — because large groups typically contain many cultures and subcultures, and variations all the way down to the family and individual level.

China is a classic example, with well over 1 billion people divided among 23 provinces, five autonomous regions, and four direct-controlled municipalities, and shaped by differences in geographic location, natural conditions, pace of economic development, and history. There is no single monolithic "Chinese" culture; each province has a distinct cultural flavor, and there are additional subcultures to consider well beyond that level. The character of Chinese people, including social customs and ways of doing business, varies, so an executive exposed to one region's cultural norms and mores cannot assume they are ready to do business everywhere in China. (Or, worse, assume that what they learned in one Chinese province can be applied to *all* Asian people!)

People with traditional mindsets tend to find this frustrating. If they've put real effort into learning how to do business in one country or with one prominent workforce group, they may bristle at the suggestion that they must continue learning about yet more cultures and subcultures to be effective. Those with a deeper global mindset are more naturally oriented toward a continuous learning model and typically possess a better developed capacity to discern and appreciate subtle nuances within other cultures. That sensitivity and willingness to always go deeper greatly improves the chances of successful communication, negotiation, and leadership.

Adjusting Your Cultural Lens

One of the most fundamental challenges to succeeding with today's global, diverse workforce is that leaders, even at the very top of the organizational hierarchy, must be willing to adjust their own "cultural lens." In other words, they can't simply look at their workforce, or at business in general, from the perspective of their own cultural values and expectations. To see people clearly and lead them effectively, 21st century leaders must try to adjust their lens to factor in the cultural frameworks that influence people who are different from them.

This is exactly what enables leaders with a global mindset to capitalize on the strengths of a multi-racial, ethnically diverse, multi-generational workforce. Because they set aside their preconceptions and stereotypes, they get a fresh, clear view of the richness of ideas brought forward by disparate "others." Since they are thus drawing from a larger, more diverse pool of talent and thinking, increased innovation is a natural result. Because different individuals in the workforce feel "seen" for who they are and encouraged to exercise their different strengths rather than suppress them to assimilate, morale, productivity, and other performance measures improve as well. This is in sharp contrast to those leaders who try to force everyone to see, and be seen, through one cultural lens: theirs.

I should acknowledge, however, that adjusting the cultural lens can become tricky — yet even more critically important — when trying to understand and appreciate the diversity of the many individuals who are part of multiple affinity groups. For example, people who identify as LGBT do not all have the same issues or challenges. Someone from a well-off, accepting, liberal background in the U.S., for example, cannot be viewed with the same lens as someone who is an immigrant or first-generation American from a traditional culture with a strong religious heritage. Particularly with a global workforce, the national and cultural perspectives must be factored in, understood, and respected alongside identifiers like age, gender, or sexual orientation.

Next Steps: Developing and Applying a Global Mindset

As an employee, peer, and consultant I have had the pleasure of working with many extremely intelligent senior executives. In the last section I distinguished leaders with a global mindset from those constrained by rigid views, emphasizing how a global mindset is superior in succeeding with today's (and tomorrow's) diverse, global workforce. The reality, however, is rarely that cut and dried. Some executives have a global mindset in general, but may not apply it as effectively as they could, or have blindspots in certain areas. Similarly, I have seen executives who cringed at the mention of a "global mindset" still do a great job of expanding their perspective once they understood the value and saw what "global mindset" *means* in real-world contexts. With that in mind, let's review some more tangible ways that you can exercise a global mindset — and reap the rewards.

Globalize Your Evaluation of Internal and External Environment

The pace and scope of workforce diversification, and of globalization in general, mean that what constituted your "environment" a decade ago (or even a few years ago) may now represent just a *fraction* of what needs to be evaluated as part of strategic decisions. You may be running a manufacturing company in Detroit, for example, but your suppliers, competitors, and markets increasingly may be outside the U.S. Similarly, your workforce probably includes an ever-expanding range of cultures and subcultures. If you fail to take into account these new elements of the environment, your strategies will be based on incomplete and perhaps erroneous information and assumptions.

Consider something as fundamental as a SWOT analysis. What was defined as a "strength" in the more homogeneous workforce of the past may now be seen as a potential weakness. From talent strategy to marketing to capital investment, new interdependencies, patterns and cultural variables must be part of any successful analysis. In this sense, a global mindset is about constantly expanding your vision in order to fully and clearly see the constantly expanding corporate landscape. Today's executives must take into account what is happening in the world. Social and historical trends, demographic and labor developments, and market changes happening far from your headquarters have very real impacts that can't be ignored when evaluating your organization and planning for its future success.

Assume Increasing Complexity and Non-linear Relationships

The globalized environmental scanning recommended above will inevitably reveal daunting levels of complexity in almost every area of business. Technology, ease of travel and shipping, sociopolitical trends toward removing barriers to trade and investment, and the instant worldwide communication of the Internet all combine to magnify that complexity. Companies, people and indeed whole countries and economies are more deeply and densely interconnected than at any time in history, with new connections (linear and non-linear) proliferating at an incredible pace.

Leaders with a global mindset not only see this existing complexity, they are betting, correctly, that everything will become *more* complex in the years ahead. That assumption puts them in a better position to anticipate and respond to both current and future manifestations of complexity. Supply chain relationships are one obvious area where most executives have some experience in how this plays out. We've all seen examples where failing to understand, manage or anticipate the impact of *every* link in a complex supply chain had terrible consequences.

There is no point in idealizing "simpler times" when you focused on a few high-priority relationships within a clearly defined competitive niche. In a global economy, leaders must actively take steps to manage a constantly expanding array of relationships with increasingly diverse stakeholders: global talent, suppliers, investors, and customers. Companies that can't manage complexity, and turn it to advantage, will be supplanted by competitors who can.

Anticipate and Adapt — Continually

Being able to predict and respond to future business scenarios is not a new leadership skill. What is new, at least in degree, is that predictions can no longer be rooted only, or even primarily, in past experience. Increasingly, the success of prediction and response also depends on a leader's willingness and ability to explore beyond the immediate horizon — to ask questions and assess possibilities outside traditional boundaries and immediate concerns.

Many corporations are so focused on how to achieve quarterly or annual goals that they never give enough attention to positioning themselves for longer term success. I have found this to be especially true in the area of talent. If we think about the changing workforce for example, there needs to be a larger vision and plan for attracting and developing talent that incorporates the real demographic and cultural changes that can be seen coming years down the road. Unfortunately, the tendency is to make decisions based on what the workforce looks like, and what the company needs from it, today without factoring in how different everything may be three or five or ten years from now.

This brings up an important point in terms of organizational culture as well as personal leadership. Coping with the change and complexity of the global business environment is not just about reaction time or mitigating risk or even being a step ahead of competitors with a specific innovation. Rather, it's about building a general capacity, in yourself, your people, and the organization, to adapt *continuously*. In such a "learning organization," mistakes are quickly transformed into improvements instead of punished, and there is a natural focus on identifying and capitalizing on emerging opportunities. A global mindset, in this respect, is about orienting yourself and your company toward proactively creating the future instead of just reacting to it.

I cannot emphasize enough how important senior executives are in setting the tone to create that kind of learning organization. If executives model a curious nature, and are clearly life-long, active learners with an openness and excitement about new developments, these qualities filter down through the organization. The result is that there is less stress about the inevitable uncertainty, ambiguity and disruption in today's business environment and greater capacity for insight and development of creative solutions.

Invest in Talent and Talent Networks

As noted before, the new economic era is marked by a shift from fixed assets to human assets. Talent has become a primary value driver and differentiator. A global mindset toward talent is imperative — not only to better manage a diverse, global workforce, but also to expand how we define, develop and invest in talent. This isn't just about the number of bodies hired to fill defined roles; investing in talent means expanding the capacity for production and innovation *of* those bodies.

This investment is every bit as important as R&D, upgrading machinery and facilities, improving processes, and so on. Increased focus on talent — including multicultural talent — is not a nicety but a *necessity* for competing in the global economy.

A book like this can only scratch the surface in describing what that investment should look like, and the most effective approaches will vary depending on the workforce and organizational objectives. However, there are three general areas where every company should make sure it allots sufficient time, money and resources. First, with Baby Boomers entering retirement, and higher workforce turnover becoming a fact of life, it is important to have processes in place to pre-serve and pass on institutional knowledge. Second, connecting individuals and groups across functional and professional boundaries by implementing a top-notch mentoring program consistently enhances value in multiple ways, including better retention of talent. Third, a global mindset in this area should include looking at establishing and supporting talent networks, internally and beyond the organization, to encourage development and sharing of best practices.

*   *   *   *   *

What we've just discussed covers some key external applications of a global mindset. But now let's turn our focus inward. To manage the complexities that emerge as a result of globalization and evolve as successful 21st century leaders, today's executives must develop a global mindset across five dimensions: Global Business Acumen Capital; Emotional Capital; Social Capital; Cosmopolitan Orientation; and Change Agility. Let's explore each of these in the context of the core competencies of a global leader.

Global Business Acumen Capital

What do we mean by global business acumen capital? To start with the obvious, top leaders should possess a keen understanding of global business in general, as well as the global aspects of their industry, includ-ing emerging markets and global competitors. But we're also talking about the ability to build global networks, and cognizance of the inter-dependencies necessary to global success. Global corporations are highly integrated networks of supply chain partners who must work together to satisfy the needs of global customers. Leaders must under-stand the importance of such networks and discern what actions and processes (including cultural communication issues) will drive success — or create potential breakdowns.

One way this plays out is in how leaders manage the natural tensions and conflicting demands between corporate and local priorities and requirements. When global business acumen is limited to the corporate realm, the drive for economies of scale and scope, maximum efficiencies, and standardization across the global enterprise can end up causing a backlash from local offices or suppliers. In contrast, leaders who show understanding and responsiveness regarding regional customs, needs, and demands are able to strike a balance and bridge differences in ways that ultimately result in better performance all around.

Emotional Capital

Emotional capital is as important for global executives — especially those who regularly interact with offices, suppliers, or customers around the world — as it is for any expatriate trying to function in a new host country. Certain attributes consistently prove to aid success in these situations, including high levels of cultural sensitivity, adaptability, and self-confidence.

Those who struggle or fail tend to be emotionally very "tight." They can't let go of what they know and resist absorbing what they need to learn in their new environment. Lacking flexibility, they want everything to be "like it is at home" — which creates internal frustration as well as external resistance. I have seen many U.S. executives struggle with this because, although they have other types of emotional capital, they lack sensitivity and adaptability. Qualities that may be part of their success in the U.S. — such as being very structured — become obstacles in many overseas environments where there are different expectations or cultural dimensions. (We'll look at cultural dimensions in detail in the next chapter.)

Self-confidence is also highly important. Indeed, when executives are able to tap into their self-confidence, it can help them make the stretch in terms of becoming more adaptable. With self-confidence, you realize that you can handle unknown circumstances, and figure out what you need to, including how to connect with, inspire, or lead others. Self-confidence helps you walk the talk when it comes to embracing other cultures — and also energizes and reassures the people around you — a big plus for U.S. executives who may be entering environments where their presence is, at first, disconcerting.

Social Capital

In the realm of social capital, two important and entwined attributes are key for global leaders: a collaborative orientation and the ability to build trusting relationships with stakeholders from different backgrounds and cultures. Whether with employees, supply chain partners, or customers, U.S. executives will only succeed in other countries if they have (or develop) the social capital to make it clear they recognize and consider the needs of others as well as themselves (or the corporate headquarters) and intend to establish a respectful team environment. Some of this builds on qualities we discussed before, such as cultural knowledge and sensitivity. But leaders who generate positive energy and genuinely *want* to connect with other people also have a big advantage when it comes to building sustainable trusting relationships.

Cosmopolitan Orientation

Leaders with deep local roots and traditional values can certainly go on to succeed on the global stage — but it helps if, when doing business and interacting with people from other cultures, they possess or develop a cosmopolitan orientation. In a sense, "cosmopolitan orientation" is synonymous with "global mindset." We're really talking about an openness to, and appreciation for, the world's diversity. A cosmopolitan leader actively seeks out and engages diverse values and views — and indeed sees that they are essential to problem-solving and innovation. This is in contrast to leaders with "local" mindsets who only want to interact with people much like themselves, or who demand that the "others" assimilate to their values and views. If you think about it, the cosmopolitan orientation dovetails with many other qualities we've been discussing: if you are open to different cultural experiences and constantly looking to explore, learn, and evolve, then you will naturally develop cultural intelligence and sensitivity, inspire trust, and facilitate collaborative relationships and environments.

Change Agility

The last internal attribute I want to mention in terms of developing a global mindset is "change agility" — which brings us full circle with what we talked about at the beginning of this chapter. Here, however, we are focusing specifically on agility with respect to change. Leaders who are more agile in their ability to forecast, respond to, and implement change will be far more successful in leading organizations through the complexities of the global business environment. Change is here to stay, so leaders need to become proactive sponsors of change rather than being resistant or merely reactive.

Leaders who are successful in implementing corporate change have a few things in common. For one thing, their agility is entwined with a commitment to driving business excellence through the realization of corporate business strategy. As a result, they become active and visible sponsors leading and facilitating change. This includes involving other employees early in the planning process, and SWOT or other analytic approaches to make sure there is a clear understanding of the company's present situation, capabilities, challenges, and underlying mindsets that must change for the transformation to succeed.

There is a wealth of literature on change management, and notable exemplars like Motorola, General Electric and Nissan-Renault. The cultural and workforce aspects of change management are areas that merit their own book — and indeed this is one of the projects on my development board!

We've covered a lot of ground in this chapter, both in building the case for embracing a diverse, multicultural workforce and in exploring the agility and global mindset needed to do so successfully. As I will continue to emphasize throughout the book, your ability to understand and harness global talent will generate many benefits: differentiation from competitors, new perspectives to drive problem-solving and innovation, better alignment with a global customer base (and therefore higher customer satisfaction), and more.

This chapter laid the groundwork for becoming the kind of leader who can achieve those benefits. In the next chapter, I want to look at one of biggest challenges to success: a reliance on stereotypes rather than genuine understanding when it comes to different cultures. This can be especially difficult for executives who are entering cultures to which they may not have had much exposure. Simply put, we will have limited success (or no success) in interactions with employees, suppliers, and customers from other cultures until we cast off stereotypes and acquire real knowledge of what makes them tick.

I should emphasize that, coming from a very different culture, I have nonetheless developed great appreciation for existing American values, which are, after all, the product of many generations of immigrants molding together their diverse strengths and values. However, believing that these values are the "only" values is not only inaccurate, it is a sure path to failure on the global stage.

Gather up your agility and your global mindset, and let's move forward in developing "cultural intelligence" — the knowledge of how people from different cultures define loyalty, what they look for from leaders, what impacts their personal and professional interactions, and much more.

CHAPTER 3

Moving from Cultural Stereotyping to Cultural Intelligence

Many of corporate America's challenges with a multicultural workforce have the same root cause: the unquestioned assumption that other cultures should *assimilate* to the corporate culture.

There are several problems with this approach. First and foremost, it is unrealistic to expect a person to downplay or jettison their most deeply held values and customs. In most cases, what comprises an individual's culture has been with them their entire life — they can't instantly remake their identity to fit a corporate culture just because they start a new job!

Nor should we want them to. The second problem with the assimilationist approach is that it causes corporations to miss out on the wealth of new cultural nuances and insights that other cultures can *add* to the corporate culture. Yes, a distinctive corporate culture that creates a sense of community and shared identity is an important element of a high-performing organization. However, that culture should not be stagnant, and it will only be effective if it is universally embraced. By welcoming the contributions of different cultures, and actively integrating them into the organization's business framework, you assure that no one feels excluded or alienated from the corporate culture. You also enrich and strengthen your employer brand.

A third problem, and what I will hone in on for much of this chapter, is that an assimilationist mindset leads to terrible gaps of understanding about what makes diverse, global talent tick. Because "they" are expected to do all the work in assimilating themselves to the corporate culture, little or no effort is made to understand how a person's cultural background impacts their actions and behaviors.

Within today's multicultural workforce, it is inevitable that there will be great variability in communication styles, motivational drivers, management[31] (both managing and being managed), attitudes toward authority, conflict and collaboration, approaches to task completion and decision-making, and much more. Again, I will emphasize that this variability, not an insistence on conformity, will make corporate culture more dynamic and innovative, and create an inclusive environment that maximizes talent engagement and therefore overall performance. But even setting that aside, the purely practical point I am making is that you can't effectively lead or manage people without understanding them — and you can't understand them if you willfully look away from the cultural differences that make them who they are.

Prioritizing this understanding of other cultures, and tapping the power of cross-cultural synergies, must start with the executive management team. There must be a top-down commitment to letting (indeed, *expecting*) diverse, global talent to maintain their identity and contribute their own cultural hues to the big picture, rather than the assumption that they should constrain themselves within the preexisting corporate culture. As we discussed in Chapter 2, that starts with letting go of cultural stereotypes and developing a more global mindset. But it also means going a step further to truly understand different cultures and appreciate their unique qualities. It means developing what can be called "cultural intelligence."

This is true with regard to any group in your workforce, but it becomes especially critical when you have large immigrant (or first-generation ethnic) populations making up increasing percentages of your talent pool and, ultimately, becoming more and more impactful

---

[31] Author's note: It is important to remember that "management" itself is essentially a Western concept. Most research and approaches embraced in the U.S. come out of the U.S. and parts of Europe. However, more than two billion people in China and India, to cite the most prominent examples, define leadership skills and qualities differently. These "other" management styles can be quite complementary and deliver great value in the global marketplace — but only if the strengths of non-Western approaches are understood, and there is a conscious effort to match the appropriate qualities and style to the talent and situation.

on workplace performance — yet also coming from cultures with values, beliefs and preferences very different than your own. This is precisely the challenge for U.S. corporations noticing a "boom" in Asian, Middle Eastern, and Latin American talent, or opening new facilities in these regions. Relatively few U.S. executives have deep experience with these cultures, which can lead to the temptation to ignore, erase or underestimate the impact of quite significant cultural differences.

My experience in this area is both professional and personal. Given my Western education, many years working for U.S.-based organizations, and nearly two decades as a U.S. resident, I truly have a foot in both worlds. My natural mindset is to consider both Western and Eastern perspectives and to try to combine the best of my Pakistani birth culture with the best of my adopted culture. However, most U.S. executives have not had this blessing of living for many years in two very different cultures — and, even among the well-intentioned, there is a tendency to look at things only through a Western lens.

As a brief aside, one area where I see this play out again and again is in references to faith. This can be a tricky area in general, of course, but as a person of faith myself, I respect leaders who wish to acknowledge the impact of their beliefs on their life or approach to business. However, whether in meetings, corporate events, or at conferences, I am struck by how often otherwise inspiring executives reference their faith in a way that instantly alienates anyone who is not part of their particular tradition. This is unfortunate, seldom intended — and it could usually have been remedied simply by acknowledging the presence of different faiths and emphasizing parallel experiences or values rather than referencing one tradition exclusively. But, in a way, this is the categorical problem that led me to write this book: Too often, shortcomings in cultural awareness and communication end up derailing what executives are trying to accomplish.

With the growing multicultural workforce, developing and expanding one's "cultural intelligence" is becoming a prerequisite for successful corporate leadership. There are many books, systems, and consultants who can help, of course, but in this chapter I want to focus on two of the true giants in this field: Geert Hofstede and Alfonsus (Fons) Trompenaars.

Hofstede, a Dutch psychologist, conducted one of the earliest and best-known cultural studies in management, drawing data from IBM's operations in 70 countries around the world. Trompenaars, a Dutch organizational theorist, management consultant, and author in the field of cross-cultural communication, surveyed 15,000 employees in 50 countries to explore the "cultural extremes and the incomprehension that can arise when doing business across cultures." Both men created (and have constantly updated) dimensional models that make it easier to understand the basic elements of cultural differences. I recommend them, first and foremost, because their work is so extensively researched and widely accepted. On a personal level, I will also say that their work resonates for me. Again and again, I find that their insights map accurately to real-world assumptions and behaviors that mark different cultures. Importantly, their work is also accessible — I've used their concepts to great effect in both corporate and academic settings. Their work is useful in defining a framework for diversity and inclusion — and provides an excellent foundation to start building cultural intelligence.

Hofstede's and Trompenaars' numerous books are vital additions to any executive's reading list. As you will see, their ideas overlap in some respects, but also have unique insights that make it valuable to read both. Given the limited amount of space in a book like this, I just want to give you a short, but hopefully impacting, overview of the cultural dimensions that are so central to their work. I will start with Hofstede, who mapped key cultural characteristics of the countries he studied to six value dimensions. I am going to provide just a basic scan of his work, but I encourage you to dig deeper on your own. Hofstede's dimension scores provide insightful, quantitative comparisons between different nations, and can be found online at www.geert-hofstede.eu. In the second part of the chapter I will look at six of Trompenaars' seven cultural dimensions. Here I will not only explain what the dimensions measure, but also delve into how I have seen these qualities play out both professionally and personally.

The Dimensions of Geert Hofstede[32]

Hofstede's first cultural dimension, **Power Distance**, measures the degree to which less powerful members of organizations and institutions accept the fact that power is not distributed equally. High power distance means there tend to be steep organizational hierarchies, with more autocratic leadership and less employee participation in decision-making. For example, Hofstede's power distance index shows very high scores in Latin and Asian countries, the Arab world, and much of Africa. On the other hand, most Anglo and Germanic countries have lower power distance scores. In these cultures — and certainly we see this in the U.S. — there is an acceptance, and even expectation, that more people should have "access" to power and that decision-making should be consultative and democratic.

In all the cultural dimensions we'll discuss in this chapter, I should emphasize that both sides have pros and cons, especially in the workplace. High power distance employees are likely to be very orderly and respect the chain of command, but may struggle with the expectation in U.S. corporations that even lower-level staff should contribute to, or even challenge, the decisions of their superiors. With a low power distance population, you'll have the dynamic exchanges that arise when everyone feels invited to express their opinion, but you will also have the potential chaos of too many people weighing in on every decision, including those in which they have little or no expertise.

Uncertainty Avoidance, Hofstede's second dimension, gauges the extent to which people feel threatened by ambiguous situations. Those with high uncertainty avoidance (including Japan, Argentina and France) create institutions and beliefs to minimize or avoid uncertainties, and place high priority on adhering to rituals, routines, and

---

[32] Hofstede, Geert. **Culture's Consequences: Comparing Values, Behaviors, Institutions and Organizations Across Nations**, 2nd edition. Sage Publications: 2001.

Author's note: The first five dimensions discussed in this section are taken from Hofstede's excellent book referenced above and used with permission. Comments and applications of the dimensions to the workplace are my own.

procedures. Countries with low uncertainty avoidance (U.S., U.K., India, and Denmark, to name a few) tend to emphasize flexibility and informality. In industries or areas of a corporation where there is rapid change and outside-the-box thinking is beneficial, employees from low uncertainty avoidance cultures may be the better fit. However, if you're talking about an organization with deeply established traditions or tasks that require methodical precision, you probably want someone with a high uncertainty avoidance profile.

Hofstede's third value dimension measures **Individualism vs. Collectivism**. In cultures that score high for individualism, people tend to look after themselves and their immediate family only, whereas in collectivist cultures, large extended families are very important, and affiliation with larger societal groups or organizations is an important aspect of both identity and responsibility.

This dimension shows clear gaps between most developed, Western countries and less developed, Eastern countries. North America and Europe consistently score high for individualism (e.g., 80 for Canada), while the scores of Asia, Latin America and Africa signify strong collectivistic values (13 for Colombia, 14 for Indonesia). At the extreme ends of this dimension, you have Guatemala scoring a 6 and the U.S. scoring 91. Japan and some nations in the Arab world are notable for scoring in the middle of this dimensional scale.

The next dimension in Hofstede's model is **Masculinity vs. Femininity**. In masculine cultures, material success and power are dominant values, while feminine cultures place more value on relationships and "quality of life." Most if not all U.S. executives have dealt with the challenges of balancing and bridging masculine/feminine differences in their workforce based primarily on gender. But many have not given sufficient consideration to how much whole cultures may lean one way or the other. Nordic countries, for example, have very low (feminine) scores, including Norway at 8 and Sweden at 5. In contrast, Japan's 95 makes it a very masculine culture, and European countries like Hungary, Austria and Switzerland also score high. In the Anglo world, masculinity scores are usually relatively high — the U.K. is 66, the U.S. is 63. Latin countries vary — from the predominantly masculine Venezuela at 73 to a much more feminine Chile at 28.

The fifth dimension compares **Long-term Orientation (LTO) and Short-term Orientation (STO)**. In analyzing a society's time horizon, LTO cultures attach more importance to the future. There is often a pragmatic approach based on future rewards that will come from exercising qualities like persistence, saving and capacity for adaptation. In an STO culture, the values align more with a relationship to the past and the present, including steadiness, respect for tradition, "saving face," drawing on societal experiences, and fulfilling communitarian social obligations. This is one of the newer dimensions added to Hofstede's model, so there is not as much data to drive conclusions, but, in general, East Asian countries like China, Hong Kong and Japan tend to score high (i.e., they are LTO). Anglo countries, the Muslim world, Latin America and Africa tend to score low (STO), and European countries are more in the midrange.

The last of Hofstede's dimensions, added to his model in the 2010 book, **Cultures and Organizations: Software of the Mind**, is **Indulgence and Restraint**. Here he is gauging the extent to which members of a culture (and the culture itself) focus on controlling desires and impulses (restraint) as opposed to embracing gratification of anything related to enjoying life (indulgence). Restraint-based societies, including East Asia, Eastern Europe and the Muslim world, often have strict social and cultural norms designed to curb such gratification. In indulgent cultures (scores are highest in Latin America, parts of Africa, the Anglo world and Nordic Europe), these same regulations might be seen as repressive.[33]

I'll go deeper into how cultural dimensions play out in the workplace in the next section, but I hope the takeaway from this short review of Hofstede is a deeper awareness of how impacting, and varying, cultural differences between nations can be. The old assumption that "an engineer is an engineer" regardless of national origin has been disproven. On the contrary, Hofstede's extensive data collection and

---

[33] Hofstede, Geert; Gert Jan Hofstede; and Michael Minkov. **Cultures and Organizations: Software of the Mind**, 3rd edition. McGraw-Hill, New York, NY: 2010.

rigorous analysis provide strong evidence that national culture plays a greater role in determining employee attitudes, values and behaviors than profession, education, or even gender and race.

The Dimensions of Fons Trompenaars[34]

There are similarities between Hofstede's work and that of Fons Trompenaars — including the use of paired extremes to frame a spectrum of cultural possibilities. However, Trompenaars is perhaps better known in corporate environments, since he has applied his dimensions over a long and distinguished career as a management consultant. Indeed, among other recognitions, he has been named one of the world's most influential HR thinkers by *HR Magazine*.

I'm going to look at six of the seven dimensions used in his work. A seventh, **Internal vs. External Control**, is quite interesting in its own right, but I have not found it to be as clear-cut across cultures or as easily applied as the other six in terms of the workplace.

Universalism vs. Particularism

Universalism means that there is uniform application of rules and procedures, regardless of situation, context, or the individuals involved. Particularism implies being willing (or even expected) to adjust rules and procedures depending on the situation or individuals.

The U.S., including its corporate cultures, falls on the universalist side of this dimension. However, globalization of the talent pool means that many U.S. companies now have employees from countries that have a particularist background. This fundamental difference must be factored in or there will be misunderstandings, an oversimplified

---

[34] Trompenaars, Fons, and Charles Hampden-Turner. **Riding The Waves of Culture: Understanding Global Diversity in Business**, 2nd edition. McGraw Hill, New York, NY: 1998.

Author's note: The dimensions discussed in this section are taken from Trompenaars' excellent book referenced above and used with permission. Comments and applications of the dimensions to the workplace are my own.

judgment of certain behaviors, and, ultimately, the loss of some of your best talent. For example, there will be situations where, from a universalist background, everything is a matter of black and white, but an employee from a particularist culture will be seeing shades of gray. With no malicious intentions whatsoever, they may "bend" a rule to serve what they see as a higher priority or to accommodate a superior — not realizing that, in their new corporate culture, such rule-bending is a serious breach regardless of the circumstances.

We also see this play out when U.S. companies set up operations in countries that have a particularist culture. I can think of at least one case where a large, multinational financial institution received negative news coverage and broad criticism when it was discovered that they were not following the exact same hiring practices in certain countries as they did in their U.S. operations. The universalist perspective on this was that changing the rules to fit another culture was unethical. Having worked for so long in U.S. organizations, I do understand the value of rigid hiring rules that require everyone to go through the same regimen of interviews and background checks and so on. However, coming from a particularist background, my initial reaction to what the company had done was to see it as a respectful adaptation to cultures where stature and family connections play a more prominent role in hiring decisions. (This also ties in to another of Trompenaars' dimensions, Achievement vs. Ascription, which we'll discuss later.) Having different hiring criteria, including embracing the value of family connections, does not make another country less ethical!

I want to make it clear that my point is not to come down on one side or the other. Indeed, the value of "dimensional" models like Hofstede's and Trompenaars' is that they encourage us to see both sides, and the range of possibilities in between. I would never try to convince U.S. executives to abandon their universalist ways — there is strength and value in what has evolved out of that perspective. However, I do try to get them to see that a particularist perspective can be equally valid and beneficial.

The bottom line is that, no matter where you are on the cultural dimensions, the only way forward in a global economy is for everyone to make the effort to understand each other and find the best ways to embrace, rather than erase, what makes others different. In the corporate world, that must start with leaders like you setting the tone for open, respectful communication, and the inclusion of differences — including adaptations on the part of the corporate culture — rather than a one-way demand for everyone to magically transform their values into the same value set that exists in the U.S.

Individualism vs. Collectivism

This dimension centers on whether individual rights and values are dominant or subordinate to those of society as a whole. The most individualist countries include the U.S., Canada, the U.K. and Switzerland, while nations like Japan, Pakistan, Egypt, and India embody collectivist values.

If you come from a collectivist culture, you are constantly evaluating the impact that your actions and decisions will have on social cohorts. In the workplace, team members from collectivist background often foster very close social bonds that extend beyond the work environment. This is not just a matter of co-workers developing a friendship — it is common for whole families to have significant levels of interaction, deepening the sense of shared identity and loyalty toward each other. From these bonds, it is natural to want to watch someone's back, and to be willing to make altruistic sacrifices for them or their families. Few Western executives would argue with any of these qualities, of course, but they often underestimate how deep the commitment to honoring these social bonds goes.

I have an interesting HR example from early in my career when I worked with an international financial institution in my native Pakistan. In my country, it is expected that male employees who are married and have family financial obligations (often for an extended family) will receive higher compensation than a single female with fewer financial needs, particularly if, as is the norm in many Asian and Middle Eastern cultures, she still lives with her parents. Because of that assumption, my bonus payouts were consistently lower than those of male colleagues whose performance and outcomes were at the same level. I had tremendous respect for my boss at the time, because he also emphasized his satisfaction with my work at my performance review even though, for cultural reasons, this did not translate into the monetary rewards I would have reaped as a married man. Furthermore, because I am from this culture, I did not consider this an outrage — on the contrary, it made sense to me that the company should pay more to someone who had to support an entire household (or more than one).

Now, let's be clear, I am *not* offering my fellow U.S. executives a new excuse to maintain the gender gap in salaries! My point is this: Concepts such as "pay for performance" do not always translate well for individuals, or locations, that have a collectivist mindset. Since they put familial and community obligations ahead of personal gain, they may be motivated less by the size of a bonus than by the availability of flex time to care for family members, or other non-monetary benefits.

Neutral vs. Emotional

In neutral cultures, objective analysis of situations and decisions is preferred over the integration and outward display of feelings that mark an emotional culture. It is easy to see this playing out in a diverse workforce, particularly in decision-making and communication styles. Those with an emotional orientation see subjective forms of assessment as vital to good decision-making — opinions, intuition, and gut feelings are all considered valid criteria. Those with a neutral mindset emphasize hard data and objective analysis, and may be dismissive of more subjective factors.

In neutral cultures (including Japan, Germany, Switzerland, and China) communication tends to be matter-of-fact, especially in the workplace. In the most emotional countries (Italy, France, the Middle East, Latin America, India, Pakistan) emotions are readily represented and integral to the work culture. Voice pitch and dynamics, hand gestures, and so on are seen as a natural way to enrich communication and elaborate on what is being conveyed. However, it is worth noting that most cultures on the emotional end of this dimension also tend to respect authority. In other words, incorporating emotions in communications and decision-making does not imply an unbridled free-for-all system. I am a good example of this. Although I am more comfortable being expressive than many Westerners, my natural mindset is to be deferential toward my superiors. Now, intellectually, I understand that in the U.S. it is important to push back and challenge your superiors, but I must exert a very conscious effort to do that. In fact, the very word "challenge" in my culture has a negative connotation of belligerence and disrespect.

Once again, the lesson here is that with a diverse, global workforce, you have to be agile in exercising different management styles, sensitive to different communication and motivational needs, and willing to step in and help someone find the best bridge between their native values and behaviors and the demands of their role or needs of their co-workers. Thinking about the diversity of my own direct reports, if I treated everyone exactly the same, I would inevitably be successful with a few but very ineffective with others. What works for the retired Air Force colonel who has enormous respect for authority and a fairly neutral demeanor would not work at all for the Millennials who go straight to treating everyone as a peer and seek constant recognition and emotional encouragement. Trompenaars' dimensions help us frame such differences so that we can make the appropriate adjustments to get good performance from everyone.

Specific vs. Diffuse

Are relationships and obligations limited to a specific context, such as the workplace — or do they typically extend far outside their immediate origin? This is the difference between a culture that is specific and one that is diffuse.

Countries like India, China, Japan and my native Pakistan are very diffuse cultures. During one job, my boss's wife gave me money and requested that I buy a wardrobe of clothes for their first baby during a trip abroad — and I was happy to do so. That's an example of a work relationship diffusing into a social relationship — my boss's wife felt completely comfortable making that request, and I felt only honored to oblige. But imagine that scenario in the U.S., which is a highly specific nation — it would likely cause consternation for both parties! Even much simpler requests or interactions are relatively rare.

Again, with these cultural dimensions, no right or wrong is implied, but coming from a more specific culture like the U.S. can be a disadvantage for executives when trying to understand diverse talent. To "get" who someone is, you must experience the whole of their lives, not just who they are in their role at work. But that is difficult if your culture presents few opportunities to know (and in some cases even has taboos against knowing) employees outside the office setting, relating to their familial responsibilities, and so on.

Recall in the last section that I mentioned my discomfort with challenging my superiors, but that I also understood that it was important to do so in a Western corporate culture, and so I consciously will myself to push past my initial perceptions and approaches. This is what good executives working with a multicultural workforce must do again and again — push beyond their own comfort zone and reach out to the "other" cultures. So, even though your orientation may be toward specific relationships, I urge you to make a conscious effort to be strategically diffuse, especially with your global talent!

Achievement vs. Ascription

This dimension refers to how individuals and a culture measure and communicate status. Specifically, achievement cultures tend to convey status, credibility, authority, and power based on merit. In ascription societies, qualities like family background, class, gender, and age play more important roles.

Countries where status tends to be ascribed include Egypt, Turkey, Pakistan, and Argentina (and slightly less so, Russia, Japan, and France). Cultures with more of an achievement orientation include the U.S., U.K., Canada, Norway, Sweden, and Australia. Talent from the Middle East and Latin America, as well as India and Pakistan, have an interesting blend of achievement and ascription attributes.

To illustrate how this dimension plays out, when I returned to Pakistan after completing my graduate education in the U.S., I was hired as a banker with a major multinational firm. Certainly my education (achievement) played a role in landing this position — but so did my family background and prominent family connections in business, military and civil government circles (ascription). In the U.S., you sometimes hear people say "it's not what you know, it's who you know." But because this is an achievement culture, efforts are made to combat that, and people take great pains to show that their success comes from their own effort, not family or connections. In my part of the world, the "who you know" and "what you know" are embraced as more or less equal components.

With this dimension, keep in mind that when you have talent from a more ascription-oriented culture, you cannot expect them to simply cast off that part of their character when they take a job in corporate America. The social status they bring with them is as real and important to their identity (sometimes more so) as professional accomplishments. This again highlights how important it is to get to know the people you manage beyond their day-to-day roles and most apparent skills. With talent from ascriptive cultures, you will probably find that you are better able to communicate and motivate individuals once you have taken the time to learn and acknowledge aspects of status, such as family position, that get downplayed in the U.S., but are still deeply embedded in how they perceive themselves and want to be perceived.

Sequential vs. Synchronic Time

The last of the Trompenaars dimensions I want to touch upon could not be more fundamental: time itself! There are many notable workplace repercussions from the differences between sequential cultures (experiencing time as a linear progression of events) and synchronic cultures (experiencing a more fluid sense of time that frequently involves multiple events at once). Some are obvious, such as how a person's orientation in this dimension impacts punctuality and whether attitudes toward deadlines are very literal or a little looser. People from sequential cultures, including Sweden and most northern European countries, tend to be very punctual, plan everything according to tight timetables, and if they say "we will send this report tomorrow" they mean precisely that: the next day. People from synchronic cultures, including many southern European, Latin American, Arabic and South Asian countries, see chronological precision as far less important and time as more malleable. "We will send this report tomorrow" may not mean literally the next day so much as "in the near future." Rigid adherence to a set schedule is a foreign concept, and one that would often be at odds with other priorities. For example, when I am in my native Pakistan, a synchronic culture, if I have a meeting scheduled between 9 and 10, it would not be unusual or the least bit irritating if one or more attendees did not show up until 9:15. Nor would it be unexpected if each of us at the meeting were interrupted by several things during our time together. And we would feel no pressure to end the meeting precisely at 10 just to run along in an effort to be on time for our next appointment. It would feel illogical, and worse in my country, inhospitable, to break up a meeting when there were clearly more things to be said or done.

In the U.S., the synchronic approach tends to be seen as problematic. Certainly, I make a conscious effort to respect the values of my sequential peers by paying closer attention to meeting times than I would if I were in Pakistan. This is one of those basic areas where a little explanation and coaching will usually help someone from a different culture to adjust their inner clock accordingly, at least during work hours.

However, there is another, often overlooked manifestation of the synchronic mindset that can be a tremendous advantage: People from synchronic cultures are accustomed to juggling a range of issues simultaneously. In other words, they are natural multi-taskers who do not get frazzled when several projects all require attention with competing deadlines. Compared to Western colleagues, this has been one of my professional strengths. Where peers sometimes get overwhelmed if not able to focus on one task at a time, I actually thrive when given multiple tasks and can be relied on to complete them successfully.

As with all the dimensions, each of the polar attributes has both advantages and disadvantages. Once again, I will emphasize that the usefulness of these dimensions is that they liberate us from believing that the workplace, or co-workers, or ourselves, must be only one way. On the contrary, the dimensions teach us to recognize a broader spectrum of possible strengths, which then allows us to match those strengths to the appropriate situation. That is really at the heart of any successful global talent strategy.

Building on the Dimensions

The cultural dimensions of Hofstede and Trompenaars provide tremendous insights and a strong foundation for building cultural intelligence. But they are the start, not end, of an ongoing process to deepen your understanding of the cultural differences of people you lead and manage. There are a plethora of more specific issues that merit close attention when it comes to global talent. To round out this chapter, I will highlight two that are especially important to many of the cultures at the forefront of today's global talent: saving face, and allegiance to family. Unfortunately, these areas are sometimes misunderstood and their impact underestimated in the U.S.

"Saving face" or honor or pride is important in one way or another in almost all cultures. It can include a range of elements: status, respect, power, insider/outsider relations, and even humor. However, it is critical to realize that what defines or threatens "face," strategies for maintaining or protecting or redeeming it, and other dynamics can play out quite differently across cultures.

To get a good insight into this, let's return to our cultural dimensions. Recall that both Hofstede and Trompenaars had an Individualism/Collectivism dimension. For those who see themselves as self-determining individuals, and do not consider an extended group to be central to their identity, "face" is, logically enough, usually about preserving a personal image — for oneself as much as with others. This dovetails with the belief that one can and should exert control in situations to achieve chosen goals that, again, are usually primarily personal. "Saving face" may take the form of a highly competitive stance in negotiations or confronting anyone who is perceived as committing a wrong against you or disrespecting you. All of this is considered "standard" behavior in the U.S.

However, if I am from a culture where my primary identification is as a group member, and as having a particular place in that group, then "face" invariably revolves more around group perceptions than self-assertion. Indeed, direct confrontation or highly individualistic approaches to problem-solving may be eschewed for fear that they would disturb the harmony of the community or reflect poorly on a person's group. For people with this cultural orientation, saving face may include avoiding criticism of others. The downside of this is that immediate disappointment or anger that has been repressed may later come out in more damaging ways. Another common strategy is to avoid direct conflict by having a third party intervene and serve as a go-between for the affected parties. If handled well, this can actually be very effective in saving face while minimizing potential damage to relationships, group dynamics, or larger networks.

Getting back to our multicultural workforce, saving face is an especially critical need for people from traditional Eastern cultures. Socially, including in work relationships, it is closely entwined with concepts like respect for superiors and reverence toward one's elders. The considerable talent pool emerging from these cultures exhibits a high degree of respect toward those above them in the leadership hierarchy — and expects the same in return from subordinates. This has pros and cons of course depending on the situation. Some U.S. executives want those they manage to be more confrontational, and, as I pointed out before, among younger generations in the West, there is a tendency for even entry-level employees to go immediately to treating everyone as a peer.

My advice here is, first and foremost, to be mindful of these differences when you have talent, including upper management, that comes from a more collectivist orientation. So long as everyone is conscious of the differences in saving face and negotiating power dynamics, all sides can find ways to adapt and work together effectively. Always keep in mind that, depending on the context, challenging someone's point of view (or asking them to challenge yours), even in the spirit of Western concepts like "a healthy debate" or "constructive criticism," can be construed as overly confrontational and disrespectful. It's important to be aware of, and to avoid, pushing people in ways that could put them at risk of losing face.

The other social characteristic that defines much of today's global talent is allegiance to family. In most Asian and Latin American culture, there is not only a very deep sense of obligation to one's family, the very definition of "family" is usually broader than what you may be used to in the U.S. One's parents, in-laws, siblings, and even cousins may fall under your "family" responsibility. Those who emigrate to the U.S. for professional reasons do not leave those obligations behind. On the contrary, the sense of obligation, and desire to fulfill it, may actually increase because of the lack of support structures found in the U.S.

Additionally, these cultures deign it totally inappropriate and callous to put elderly parents in assisted living establishments — the expectation, and desire, is that they will become caretakers of their elders.

These greater family obligations may put an employee in difficult or impossible situations as they try to keep up with commitments at work. Too often, the approach is to say, well, that's their problem. I argue for the opposite approach, not only because it is more humane, but because it makes better business sense. If you help people meet their family obligations, by offering flex time or work-from-home options for example, you will gain a far more productive and loyal employee. It is important to note that this shouldn't just cover the most dramatic examples like a spouse with cancer. For people with extended family obligations, they may truly need a couple hours to help an uncle who doesn't speak English very well get through a basic doctor's appointment. No one should be made to feel guilty or have to go through long explanations in order to do what is right within their sense of family obligations. Instead, make a point of showing that you respect allegiance to family and that you trust people to get work done in a way that fits with the rest of their life.

The New Talent Management Paradigm: Reverse Acculturation and Whole Employee Rewards

The diverse, global workforce makes it more important than ever to understand how values, beliefs, work and communication styles, and other dynamics vary among different talent groups. In the next chapter, I will talk about the fact that "diversity" is not enough to succeed — you must become an authentically inclusive corporate culture to attract and retain today's best global talent. Understanding is an important first step toward inclusion, and hopefully the dimensions, examples and tips provided in this chapter will feed both your desire and your capacity to understand those from other cultures.

At root, this comes back to a concept I touched upon earlier: reverse acculturation. The old "they should assimilate to our way of doing things" mindset is simply not viable. The bridge joining different cultures cannot be a one-way street! Reach out to those with differences, invite their contributions to the overall culture, and show your own ability to adapt — and you will inspire the same. Expect your talent to make all the adaptations and sacrifices, and you will end up with a growing pool of potential high-performers who instead become less motivated, less loyal, and less innovative — because you have forced them to be less *themselves*.

In terms of the nuts and bolts of talent management strategy, the corollary here is that Total Rewards programs must expand, and become more flexible, to appeal to the broader range of values, interests and obligations in today's talent pool. The specifics of such programs are best left to each individual company, since they must align with your workforce. I do recommend that, in assessing your workforce and designing new programs or initiatives, at least some of the decision-makers be *from*, or have deep personal experience with, other cultures.

However, there is one more general principle that can be applied to any company, workforce or situation: aligning talent management with the *whole* employee. What does this mean? Let's go back to our discussion of family obligations. New talent management strategies cannot only look at a person as an "employee" and focus on what can be controlled and cultivated and rewarded in the workplace. They must instead be based on a view of "employment" as just one aspect of a person's "whole" being. In the case of much global talent, that "whole" will also include the family and social obligations woven into the fabric of who they are. Again, that plays out practically in executives and managers offering more latitude in how employees balance their work responsibilities with family care. As an aside, I am constantly struck by how many companies readily provide time off and other rewards for employees to engage in community services to help strengthen the company brand. Yet, little or no help or credit is given to those whose "service" involves their own families!

Here are a few more quick ideas for moving toward a talent management strategy that addresses the whole person:

- **Customize work plans to give individuals greater flexibility in managing their work.** Move from "making sure butts are in seats" to inviting employees to help determine how and when they can be most productive.

- **Base policies and options on a deeper (and more diverse) understanding of personal career aspirations, family needs, social values, and so on.** Ask what will make this person leave a job and find ways to avoid those scenarios. Ask what will inspire individuals — and then implement it. Accept that the answers will be different for different individuals. "One size" will always be the *wrong* size!
- **Personalize the talent management process.** Have frequent discussion opportunities, and create talent intelligence profiles to keep relevant managers up to date on employee needs.
- **Transition from monitoring to empowering employees.** Sick days are one very practical example where this is needed. Trust your employees to take the sick days they need, and avoid systems that invite distrust on all sides.
- **Be more generous in vacation policies.** With a global workforce, there are very practical reasons for this — employees literally need more days in order to travel and visit with family. However, this approach has benefits for the entire workforce. Time away from work serves the "whole" person, and enables them to bring more of their strength back to work.

Some of today's top companies are already well along in implementing this approach. SAS is one that has developed a stellar reputation for putting a premium on talent and providing very robust and attractive benefits: free concierge services, free onsite breakfasts and lunches, subsidized day-care centers and summer camp, dry cleaning, car detailing, a UPS depot, a book exchange, a meditation garden, an in-season tax-prep vendor, an orthotics store — the list goes on and on!

Now, I recognize that not all companies can afford to provide benefits that extensive, but all companies can and *should* be taking steps in that direction. Doing so will sharpen the competitive edge that talent can provide. I know that change can be hard. But if you stay stuck in the same approaches and programs that have been used for 20 or 30 years, you will still experience change — unfortunately, it will be the constant change of "revolving door" talent turnover and an erosion of your employer brand and market position.

CHAPTER 4

Moving from Diversity to Inclusive Behavior

Throughout Part 1 of this book I have frequently used the words diversity and inclusion. I have also emphasized that they are not synonymous. Diversity in the workplace is not enough — you must create a culture of truly *inclusive* behavior to leverage the value and competitive advantages offered by diverse, global talent. To reinforce the critical importance of this point, I want to devote an entire chapter, albeit a short one, to exploring how to make sure your organization does not "stall out" on the road from diversity to inclusive behavior.

To be clear, there are still areas where a conscious investment in diversity is the necessary focus. Even in fairly progressive organizations with very diverse workforces, for example, the leadership pipeline may lack diversity. However, diversity can no longer be narrowly defined as a compliance issue or even a humanistic imperative. As the demographics and trends we discussed in Chapter 1 indicate, in more and more organizations, a diverse workforce is not an "accomplishment," it is simply a *reality*. The talent pool itself has diversified and globalized, so that businesses of sufficient size and market reach will *inevitably* have a workforce that includes professionals from diverse national and cultural backgrounds, spanning three or four different generations, and bringing a widening range of personal and group-defined values and behaviors to the workplace.

The notion of a homogeneous corporate culture has become obsolete, and counterproductive as a goal. Wisely embraced or obstinately resisted, the new talent reality is that almost every corporate culture is becoming a rich mosaic of human diversity where cultural non-conformity and individualized expression are the rule rather than the exception. Indeed, even the meaning of "diversity" is diversifying, as more subcultures find and express their own identity, ethos and ideas in the workplace.

This is good news — diversity is proving beneficial for innovation, in decision-making processes, and as a reflection of, and connection to, the reality of diverse global markets. However, diversity does not deliver its full value overnight or without effort by the management team. On the contrary, developing new talent management strategies and programs that align with a diverse workforce is essential. Such strategies and programs will vary depending on the specifics of your workforce and organization, but to be successful they must all have one thing at their center: inclusive behavior.

Inclusive behavior means we aren't just hiring people from different backgrounds, we are proactively taking steps to *include their differences* in a dynamically evolving corporate culture which encourages them to express those differences. That starts with creating an organizational climate that acknowledges and appreciates difference. Cultural diversity training and programs that promote cross-cultural networking are a good start, but ideally, we want to go far beyond this. Day-to-day integration is key, and informal efforts can be just as important as formal programs in tapping diverse skills and perspectives and ensuring high levels of engagement, collaboration and cross-cultural understanding. For example, in understanding and appreciating the "other" there is no substitute for direct experience. As valuable as the cultural dimensions from the last chapter are, or the insights that come through formal training, one of the best ways to "get" what motivates someone from another culture, what they value, how they communicate, and so on, is to spend time with them and ask them.

Once again, I must emphasize the critical role leaders have in this respect. Indeed, this is why I am writing a book primarily for executives, boards, and management teams, rather than a manual for a general audience. Your success (or failure) in adopting an inclusive mindset and modeling inclusive behavior — in everyday interactions as well as investment in inclusion programs — has an enormous ripple effect throughout the organization. Obviously, decisions that senior executives make with regard to talent management strategy, cultural change, communications, and so on also drive the "talent brand" or "employer brand" — e.g., whether or not you are perceived as an inclusive employer in the marketplace.

With that in mind, let's turn to a few "executive development" areas that will help you be an inclusive leader who is adept at managing and motivating the diverse workforce of today and the future — and able to transform the tremendous potential of global talent into the reality of a high-performing organization.

Defining Corporate Culture Around Inclusive Behavior, Not Assimilation

When it comes to diversity, and especially achieving a culture of inclusive behavior, the executives who struggle the most invariably suffer from what might be called "corporate conformity syndrome." This syndrome includes a host of perceptions and behaviors that all revolve around a fundamental belief that corporate culture should be homogeneous, unchanging, and primary. Consequently, the onus is on "outside" cultures to assimilate — to erase (or at least suppress) what makes them different and learn to "do things our way."

I would question whether this model was ever truly effective. But, setting that debate aside, the increased diversity in the workforce, combined with shifting social expectations about the relative rights of employers and employees, make it impossible to "go back" to the days of having, and enforcing, a monolithic corporate culture. Efforts to do so are a terrible waste of resources, and a drain on morale for the ever-growing segment of the workforce that doesn't feel a native kinship with that culture. Perhaps worst of all, this approach undermines the strengths and value that a more diverse workforce can bring to the organization. Instead of having employees who provide a constant influx of new ideas, perspectives and insights, you end up with employees who are always "holding back."

A singular, static corporate culture cannot adequately serve or contain the diverging values, work styles, motivations and needs of a workforce that includes more and more immigrants, people of color, women, multiple generations, LGBT and other distinct groups. The realities of globalization and cross-border communications make such a culture a serious disadvantage in other areas of business operations as well. Whether we are talking about selling to new markets, partnering with suppliers and vendors in other regions, or building a viable international brand presence, the bottom line is that the corporate culture must look and feel more like the diverse range of audiences that the organization interacts with on a regular basis. The way to do that is to fight any latent tendencies to want or demand assimilation, and instead have a culture that not only makes room for differences but indeed is defined *by* those differences.

Reverse Acculturation and Continuous Cultural Learning

I've emphasized the importance of reverse acculturation several times, and I will touch upon it again here not only as an essential quality for a successful global leader but, increasingly, as a necessity for productivity and smooth business operations.

We can define reverse acculturation as a willingness and process of reaching out to, and adapting to, different cultures rather than demanding that they adapt to you or to the dominant culture. I think of this as having three components.

First, reverse acculturation requires a fundamental orientation or attitude — you must genuinely respect the validity of other cultures and individuals and be open to seeing the advantages of "their ways."

Second, reverse acculturation requires education — whether formal, informal or both. It is rare for reverse acculturation to just be your native mode of interacting. Most of us must learn to appreciate other national or ethnic cultures, LGBT or gender issues, generational differences, and so on. It is to be expected that appreciation for some differences will come more naturally than others. In this sense, your capacity for reverse acculturation can be assessed and developed just like any other competency. If you know you are having an especially hard time appreciating Millennials, for example, then that's where you look for education.

The third component of reverse acculturation is in what we do and how we do it. As managers, for example, reverse acculturation means tailoring our management and communication styles to better suit the diverse cultural nuances, perspectives and needs of those we are managing. To some degree, those familiar with the "servant leadership" approach have a headstart here. If you're already accustomed to putting the needs of others ahead of your own in order to help them develop and perform, then their cultural needs are a natural extension of that.

Sometimes, I have had people tell me that reverse acculturation feels daunting because of the sheer number of cultures and subcultures they must acculturate to. This is an understandable reaction, but it actually underscores why this must be a daily practice and mindset, not just something that takes the shape of a special group or program. In other words, if reverse acculturation becomes the expectation, then no matter how much the workforce diversifies further, you will still have the right strategy — whereas programs developed for this or that situation or group may not work at all for the next group or for specific individuals.

In essence, reverse acculturation implies a commitment — both personally and organizationally — to continuous cultural learning. That means gathering data about the experiences and perspectives of your diverse employees not only through formal education or training, but also through discussions about differences *with* diverse employees and those whose backgrounds or experiences make them cultural subject matter experts (SMEs). As I've said before, this shouldn't be limited only to workplace discussions. I strongly encourage leaders to establish relationships with people who are different, which not only shows that outreach and interest is genuine, it also facilitates engagement and exploration of issues of difference in greater depth. Such relationships can often help leaders learn about and gauge the impact of cultural inequities or other challenges in their organization.

If we go back to what we learned from Trompenaars, someone like me, who hails from a nation with a diffuse cultural dimension, has a distinct advantage here. It feels very natural to me to invite peers to visit my home for dinner, for example — and not just the handful of people I work most closely with, but any number of people who I may interact with and want to learn about. This approach is a little more of a "stretch" for executives from a country like the U.S. that tends toward the "specific" side of the specific/diffuse dimension. However, I urge you to make the stretch. You can't truly understand cultures or individuals if you interact with them only in the work environment. Inclusive behavior, and an inclusive culture, must transcend work.

Proactive Development of Diverse, Global Talent

One of the most important activities of senior leadership is to identify and develop talent, including the next generation of leaders who will replace them. An inclusive mindset is critical here. Too often, executives quickly align with those most like themselves, who it may be "easier" for them to develop and mentor. This not only results in a lack of diversity in the leadership pipeline, it also prevents different perspectives and new insights from enriching executive decision-making. In addition to getting training or consulting support if necessary to help you develop individuals who are different from you as effectively as you develop those from your own background, it can also be helpful to think about how you can increase inclusivity in these six stages of talent development:

1. Avoid stereotypes about certain groups being more or less talented or qualified for specific types of work; when prioritizing individuals for advancement, be careful to filter out any personal discomfort you may feel about developing talent that comes from a different background

2. Use inclusive criteria to identify your most promising individuals; keep in mind, for example, that over the course of the development lifecycle, cultural differences may become increasingly important as differentiators or in constituting the "best fit" in increasingly globalized environments (more on this in Part 2 of the book)

3. Empower individuals targeted for development — realizing that the "what" and "how" of empowerment will vary according to a person's cultural background and needs

4. Mentor individuals throughout their development; make an extra effort to mentor those who are different from you as closely and as effectively as you mentor those who share your background, hobbies, values, etc.

5. Engage in reverse mentoring with those being developed; with those from different cultures, this helps you deepen your own cultural intelligence while also signifying your respect for the other's culture

6. Champion individuals targeted for development and build a supportive environment for their growth and career success; again, remember that "supportive" will entail different things depending on a person's cultural background

An Inclusive Approach to Total Rewards and Talent Management

In a sense, our discussion of what executives must do to achieve an inclusive environment has followed a logical order. To make any progress toward becoming an inclusive, high-performing organization, you must first let go of the notion that everyone should assimilate to a single, unchanging corporate culture. Having done that, the next step is actively reaching out to those from other cultures through reverse acculturation. From there, you are ready to identify and support top talent in a more inclusive way. Last, but certainly not least, we must talk about how Total Rewards and related talent management programs must be adapted to reflect inclusion and better attract, develop and retain diverse talent.

Here is the bad news: there is a good chance that the status quo isn't enough. If your organization is like most, your Total Reward offerings focus almost exclusively on compensation, traditional benefits, wellness, and FMLA. An inclusive approach to Total Rewards will have to recognize that many people in today's diverse workforce are not adequately served by these "rewards" alone. In fact, an increasing percentage of workers are looking for agile leadership and corporate flexibility in these areas.

As we discussed in the previous chapter, workers from many cultures very much want "rewards" that will allow them to balance work with familial obligations, including potentially an extended family unit. Younger generations are looking for more flexible work schedules, investment in their professional development, rapid career growth and transition into their "ideal" roles. A high percentage of the workforce is interested in telecommuting — notably, three out of four of those who prefer to telecommute are men.[35] And women

---

[35] Zipkin, Nina. "Men Telecommute More Than Women, Survey Shows." *Entreneur.com*, February 27, 2014. Published online at http://www.entrepreneur.com/article/231817

rightfully seek greater visibility and advancement through the leadership pipeline, including positions in the C-Suite, and on corporate Boards and executive committees. Can you afford to ignore all these groups that already constitute a large percentage of the workforce, and will make up larger and larger blocks of it in the future?

How we manage, motivate, and measure performance and define and deliver rewards *must* expand. We can no longer depend on one approach that is generally the same across corporate cultures. On the contrary, companies are getting a competitive edge with global talent precisely by differentiating their Total Rewards approach from the "standard" offered by their competitors. Flexibility and customization to fit different cultures and individuals are key. In this area, as in many others, corporate culture must heed the clarion call: Today's talent *is* diverse, and will gravitate toward inclusive environments where their differences are appreciated and their needs accommodated.

I want to close this chapter, and Part I, with a pertinent reminder about the purpose of leadership. Yes, leadership may manifest as a title or position, and decision-making power, and control over resources, and so on. But ultimately the *purpose* of leadership involves mobilizing others to see unknown potential, take on the inevitable challenges, and achieve a shared set of goals.

Overlay that purpose with the reality of a diverse, global workforce, and I hope you can see why building cultural intelligence, establishing a culture of inclusive behavior, and developing more flexible, inclusive talent management strategies is absolutely essential. To mobilize others, you must understand what motivates them, where they need support, and how best to communicate with them. This requires the agility and global mindset that we discussed in Chapter 2, the cultural intelligence and sensitivity that we covered in Chapter 3, and the focus on inclusive behavior that we've looked at in this chapter.

The demographics in Chapter 1 reinforce that this *is* the future of the workforce. It is time to let go of old ways that are failing to work even with the current workforce, and leave off "kludging" approaches that are a poor substitute for the more fundamental changes that can position your organization to become one of the top draws for global talent. Inclusive behavior is the path to higher performance.

PART II

Aligning Talent Strategy to Today's Gems

There is an extraordinary history of immigrants adding tremendous value to the U.S. economy. Indeed, it is fair to say that previous waves of "global talent" in the late 19th and early 20th centuries were a critical driver in this nation's growth into an economic superpower.

Up to about 1960, a high percentage of immigrating workers were from Europe. There is some truth to the notion that such workers were unified with each other, and with native U.S. labor, by the core characteristics of a "Euro-American" tradition. However, there were also similarities with the challenges and opportunities presented by today's more culturally diverse workforce. First-generation workers from Italian, German, Polish, Irish, Slovak and other backgrounds all faced very real negative stereotypes, pressure to assimilate, and a lack of understanding or appreciation for their differences. However, then, as now, those differences were an important part of what made immigrant workers so valuable — the "gems" of the workforce.

I choose the word "gems" because it suggests that the workers' differences make them stand out against the background — and that they in turn *differentiate* that background, just as a real gem set in a ring differentiates the hand wearing it. It also conveys the value of these workers — but also that the value may need to be "mined and refined."

Now more than ever, "gems" *will* differentiate the organizations that know how to attract and develop them. High-performing companies are already well ahead of the curve in tapping their value. And it is not hard to see that these gems are helping to reshape the U.S. workforce and economy in even more profound ways than their predecessors.

As the demographics and emerging talent power centers discussed in Chapter 1 make clear, today's gems are no longer primarily from

Europe. Since the late 1960s there has been a shift in the demographic make-up of immigrant workers entering the U.S. In particular, we see a significant percentage of workers coming from Asian countries and settling in the western U.S. or the Northeast Corridor.

To some degree, this shift began after the Immigration Act of 1965 (also known as the Hart-Cellar Act), which allowed immigration based on both the possession of scarce skills, and on family ties to citizens or permanent residents. This created new opportunities for foreign-born engineers and other highly educated professionals whose skills were in short supply, as well as for their families and relatives. The trend eventually helped feed the growth of high-technology industries in the Silicon Valley, which in turn added to the trend's momentum. As demand for skilled labor in the region's emerging electronics industries exploded during the 1970s and 1980s, so did immigration. By 1990, 23% of Santa Clara County (the heart of Silicon Valley) was foreign-born, surpassing San Francisco County as the largest absolute concentration of immigrants in the Bay Area.[36]

These statistics also reflected broader national trends as engineers, computer scientists, and doctors from India, Pakistan, Taiwan, China and other Asian nations came to the U.S. Those job categories are significant. Unlike previous generations of immigrant workers, these gems are not primarily concentrated in labor or the service sector; many are highly educated professionals and knowledge workers who are well versed in English. Individuals from Asian countries where English is the medium of instruction, including India, Pakistan and Bangladesh, have found that they are in an especially strong position to compete for jobs — even against workers from other parts of the Western Hemisphere.

All that said, the points I want to explore in this section of the book are not limited to the gems coming from Asian rather than European backgrounds. Since many Eastern cultures emphasize educational achievement and high standards of performance, they *are* sometimes

---

[36] Saxenian, AnnaLee. "Silicon Valley's New Immigrant Entrepreneurs." Also available online at www.ppic.org/main/publication.asp?i=102. Public Policy Institute of California: 1999.

the most visible "face" of how global talent can give companies a competitive edge — and many companies are beginning to proactively focus on this talent power center. However, today's gems also come from Latin America, the Middle East, and a range of other backgrounds. In fact, a key point is that, unlike previous waves of immigration, today's foreign-born talent is in no way a monolithic cultural entity. Even within the Asian gems, there are different cultures and subcultures that bring their own unique perspectives and ethos to the workplace. When this diversity is embraced, it becomes one more way that today's gems can enrich the collective corporate experience and contribute to the achievement of excellence. But make no mistake, to reap these benefits, leaders *must* be willing and able to embrace the real differences that define these new talent groups and facilitate inclusive behavior throughout their organizations.

Aligning talent strategy — and your organizational culture — to include, support and celebrate today's gems is an important step in gaining competitive advantage through your human capital or "people power." What we learned in Part 1 of this book provides a good foundation for understanding and appreciating diverse, global talent, but now let's hone in on some specific talent strategy areas and concepts where that understanding and appreciation play out. In Chapter 5, we will look at concepts related to "mining" today's gems, including a much-needed expansion of the traditional "high potential/high performer" model of identifying and classifying talent. In Chapter 6, we will discuss ways to "refine and retain" your gems, including evolving from the "corporate ladder" paradigm to a "corporate lattice," and also assessing and adjusting your Total Rewards approach to fit a more culturally diverse workforce.

CHAPTER 5

Mining Your Gems

The critical importance of finding and developing talent should not be news to C-suite leaders. Most recognize that no business strategy can be executed without the right talent; no innovation occurs without creative, inquisitive people; and no company survives without layers of strong, vibrant leaders to lead it confidently forward. In my own experience, most are also well acquainted with the challenges of identifying, attracting and retaining top performers, raising engagement levels, and shaping future leaders.

In the present environment, the value of human capital, and the need to win the competition for *top* talent, has become all the more imperative in the U.S. due to an aging workforce and talent shortages in key areas. Simultaneously, the challenges surrounding human capital have become more complex as executives find themselves seeking and managing skilled talent from labor markets around the world.

As discussed in Chapter 2, competing in the global marketplace requires leaders at all levels to possess a global mindset. (Indeed, the corporate vision itself must globalize if companies are to remain viable.) Increasingly, greater cross-functional and cross-industry business acumen, as well as greater cross-cultural intelligence, are also vital. All of this is deeply entwined with the approach and effectiveness of your talent strategy — including how well you are able to mine and refine the "gems" defined in the introduction to Part II.

The title of this chapter specifies mining "*Your* Gems" rather than "the" gems — an important distinction. The diversification of the workforce, combined with the complexity and fast pace of change in most industries, means that what constitutes the most valuable talent can vary significantly from company to company and situation to situation. Broadly applicable credentials like education and professional certifications still matter of course, but they cannot be the end of the search criteria. To succeed, company leaders must have a clear consensus on how they define and grow talent — on who *their* gems are, and how best to develop and motivate them.

Defining your gems requires deep internal understanding of your business. But it also requires the right mindset toward talent in general. Unfortunately, one traditional framework — classifying candidates and employees as "High-Potentials" or "High-Performers" — has shortcomings in this respect. Given the complexity of today's job roles, rapid shifts in technology, frequent industry-wide disruptions, and the astounding diversity of a multigenerational, multicultural workforce, these classifications are oversimplified at best, and can be outright misleading.

That is not to say we should replace the terms altogether — but they must be supplemented to provide a more complete and accurate picture of your gems and to guide overall talent strategy. Without additional subdistinction and clarification, "High-Potential" in particular can do more harm than good. I always urge executives to exercise caution in how they, and their companies, use this phrase. For employees, it can be very demotivating to learn you are *not* a High-Potential — and too tempting to rest on not-yet-earned laurels if you're told that you are.

My critique of a narrowly applied notion of High-Potentials has a humanistic element to it. We all have "potential," and whether it is "high" or not is situational, subjective and often in flux. But that is also precisely why, from a *business* perspective, it is strategically shortsighted to define and develop talent as High-Potential without asking *for what?* Further — and this is especially relevant with global talent — you must understand what is involved in helping someone realize this "high potential." What kind of support will they need? Additional questions should be asked about whether, or how, your company will be able to *use* the potential once realized.

There is an elasticity to talent, and fluctuation in its value for a company, that depends in large part on a confluence of needed skills and roles, available opportunities, and environment. This is not a simple equation. That is why I advise going beyond the standard High-Potential/High-Performer classifications to include two more: Best-Fit, and Differentiator.

Best-Fit puts necessary context back into the identification of someone as a High-Potential or High-Performer. It means we assess talent not in a vacuum, or according to generic criteria, but rather as it relates to specific organizational roles and needs — present or future. Similarly, when we talk about a Differentiator, we are no longer limited to performance metrics that might be "gamed" successfully in a given year; we are looking at whether the individual truly transforms your workforce and sets (or has the potential to set) your organization apart from competitors.

This set of criteria for evaluating talent can play out in a variety of ways. For example, someone may be a High-Potential in that they show promise for a range of roles due to their capacity for growth, business insight, decision-making and people management. They have added value as a Differentiator if they also exhibit qualities that could *expand* any role they take, even up to the C-suite. Similarly, we may describe someone as a High-Performer because they "rate well" individually, but a Best-Fit designation conveys the additional value of contributing (and/or being projected to contribute) exactly what is needed to achieve organizational goals.

Adding Best-Fit and Differentiator criteria sharpens decision-making. Two people may qualify as equal "High-Potentials" when it comes to training, experience and past performance, for instance. But if one is *also* a Differentiator or a Best-Fit, and the other is not, it can shed light on who to develop or promote.

Of course, arriving at a more accurate, strategically relevant definition of talent — of *your* gems — is just one step. Seeing who your Best-Fits and Differentiators are, or where there are gaps in these areas, also adds clarity to how companies need to develop and retain top talent, what growth opportunities to provide, how Total Rewards and recognition programs must be structured to drive performance, and so on.

All of this is particularly important with today's (and tomorrow's) diverse, global workforce. Among other things, it can help justify necessary investments to adequately address cultural differences in the workplace so that you will be able to mine and refine your gems effectively. And, of course, the very definition of "effective" shifts depending on who we are trying to be effective with, and what makes them tick.

Best-Fit and Differentiator criteria can also help companies avoid two mistakes that constrain the success of many talent strategies: giving too much weight to directly parallel experience, and assuming that geographic and cultural proximity is always an advantage.

To illustrate this, imagine you lead a mid-size health insurer looking to hire a new marketing VP. The traditional framework immediately hones in on a 40-something candidate who has spent his whole career in the industry, including a decade as a manager and then director with an organization like yours in another part of the country. As a bonus, this candidate was born and raised in the metro area where your company is headquartered. In the initial round of meetings and interviews, everyone agreed that he "fits right in."

But — let's take a step back. Is "fits right in" synonymous with your organization's Best-Fit strategic needs? On the surface, his career trajectory may classify him as a High-Potential for this position and, down the road, even Senior VP, but is he a *Differentiator* who can help your company adapt in an industry undergoing profound paradigm shifts? If you've taken the time to define Best-Fit and Differentiator criteria, some of this candidate's surface "strengths" may actually be liabilities compared to other candidates. A Millennial with cross-industry experience in retail, for example, may be a better Differentiator in terms of not being attached to "the way it's always been done" and introducing fresh insights and tactical approaches that will match the increasingly consumer-driven marketplace. And if your workforce and markets are diversifying — as most are — the *Best-Fit* candidate may be one who reflects changing demographics rather than one who simply mirrors the existing leadership team.

For most executives reading this book, the talent scenarios will be more complicated than this quick example — but that underscores the importance of a strategically rigorous approach. Unless your "talent lens" is adjusted to focus on strategic Best-Fits and Differentiators, you will miss opportunities to hire and develop the people who will give you a competitive edge.

Defining Best-Fits and Differentiators demands deep consideration of where your organization is, what is happening with markets and competitors, and, most importantly, how your company must evolve to succeed in the future. Last year's High-Performers may not be the Best-Fits for tomorrow's tasks. The experience that was an indicator of High-Potentials in the past may become obsolete. Similarly, hiring "local" in an effort to preserve cultural homogeneity is a terrible mistake — in a global economy, the goal should be to proactively expand the corporate culture, and aggressively mine the entirety of the diverse, global workforce.

Many of today's top companies are finding that the most effective talent strategy is both industry-agnostic and location-agnostic. There is greater focus on an individual's talent, accompanied by more flexibility, or even creativity, in envisioning how that talent can bring value to the company. Indeed, more companies are tailoring opportunities (or even entire roles) to fit an individual's strengths, rather than simply assessing "strength" in relation to a predefined job description.

Strategically, a more global background is one individual strength that should be given weight in guiding talent decisions. My work as a consultant and as an executive are an example of this. Although some of my clients, and my most recent employer, may be "national" companies, they are dealing with the reality of a global workforce and multicultural consumer base. My value to them is therefore not merely my educational background and related professional experience, but also my *cultural* experience.

I want to touch on two more points about "potential" and "performance" before closing this chapter with a few short tips to help you identify, attract and develop your gems. First, if we are going to evaluate potential, or categorize someone as a High-Potential, our focus must be on their capacity for *future* performance, not their past performance. When we do this, one quality that takes on particular value is evidence of being an active learner (one who seeks out information) rather than a passive learner (one who requires information to be pushed to them). In environments where rapid change is a fact of business, you must have talent that is adaptable, constantly trying to learn, eager to tackle new challenges, and, in many cases, adept at collaborating across both functional and cultural differences. This is what active learners bring to the table — as well as a mindset that naturally looks for innovative possibilities.

The other thing I want to emphasize is that there is no absolute correlation between "performance" and "potential" — a point too often missed when talent is being evaluated. Yes, performance in a certain type of work can be a reasonable indicator of potential to do more of that type of work. But it may not be a primary indicator, or an indicator at all, of success in other roles. It is wonderful to have a High-Performer on your team, but that does not make them a promising High-Potential — much less a Differentiator or Best-Fit — when it comes to *leading* the team. This is a common mistake that can become readily apparent when, for example, someone who has excelled in the sales function is promoted to a position of leadership, but lacks critical qualities for their new role: the ability to work well with other team members or departments, good "people" skills, emotional and cultural intelligence, and so on.

An employee's potential, or growth trajectory, must be gauged against the skill areas necessary for the future position, not current or past job responsibilities. This is why a good HR executive will push hard to identify and define the critical competencies which will determine success in a given role. One benefit of this approach is that it opens up new possibilities for cross-functional and cross-departmental movement of talent. Instead of pushing High-Performers along a linear path that may eventually put them in role where their strengths are no longer strengths, the focus is on the fundamental competencies that will facilitate high performance.

What we have been talking about so far has an enormous impact on how we define, place and promote talent. It can be especially important when assessing the complex variables at play in a more diverse, globalized workforce. However, these concepts also impact what areas and tactics should be focused on in *developing* talent.

We'll look at talent development strategy in more depth in the next chapter. Here, I will just note that few companies pay adequate attention to determining the most effective talent development tactics. Even with the High-Potentials being groomed as future leaders, development sometimes borders on being haphazard. There are no agreed upon best practices. Selection criteria are confusing or non-existent. And, perhaps worst of all, the tendency to focus development efforts primarily on a few High-Potentials leaves many other talented individuals and core contributors feeling excluded and demoralized.

There are two components to turning this around: first, creating a culture of "talent development," and second, using the best tactics to operationalize that culture. Establishing a talent development culture requires attention and effort in four areas:

- Align development programs with both corporate strategy and the needs of the workforce. Avoid cookie cutter approaches that may have been effective at other times or in other organizations but are not well suited to your present environment. As with any element of culture, authenticity is key. Talent development should feel "right" to all those involved. Keep in mind that a diverse, global workforce will include individuals and groups whose development needs may be different from those you've experienced in the past.

- Cultivate an organization-wide mindset where executive involvement in developing talent is the norm, and managers at all levels have "people development" accountability metrics built into their performance evaluation and compensation.

- Maintain a high level of transparency in talent discussions, from the lowest pay grade up through succession planning. Companies are often reluctant to acknowledge which individuals have been identified as having "high growth potential" because of concerns that it could lead to unhealthy internal competition or stifle collaboration. However, lack of transparency and clarity tends to have worse repercussions, including diminished credibility and trust in the talent development process.

- Development efforts should be holistic, appealing to and strengthening both the cognitive and emotional sides of an individual's personality. In addition to being more effective for the individual, this approach will also help deepen commitment, and improve the adoption and success of specific strategies and tactics.

With the right talent mindset and development culture in place, the next question is what tactics will best operationalize the culture. That will depend on your industry, environment, and workforce, so I won't go into too much detail (until we are working side by side!) — but, in general, tactics should:

- Introduce rigorous candidate selection criteria that combine nominations and objective assessments. This is where Best-Fit and Differentiator criteria can play an important role. This approach may require a little extra time upfront, but it pays off big in helping you avoid wasting resources on the wrong people, or having too many people "wash out" early and need to be replaced.

- Include managerial goals and measurement of their people's success in acquiring and applying new skills. This is always the right approach, but it becomes even more critical to have this hands-on involvement and accountability when managers are dealing with a diverse, global workforce. Without frontline goals and measurement, it is easy for development to go off track when managers are dealing with people who have different cultural values and motivations.

- Integrate rotational opportunities to expose top talent to other business units, geographies, and product or service lines. This should not be "movement just for the sake of movement" — it must match individual and department goals. But, planned thoughtfully, such assignments will broaden the individual's experience, while also delivering payback to the organization through cross-pollination of ideas and best practices. Recalling our previous discussion about the value of cross-functional and cross-industry experience, keep open to the possibility of extending rotational opportunities even outside of the organization to related industries or nonprofits. The latter can have a positive impact on your company's overall brand image while also helping to retain talent by giving them a chance to deepen their sense of belonging and contribution to the larger community.

Too many of today's talent gems are not being seen clearly because of outdated talent strategy frameworks. In my experience, it is common for as much as a quarter of a company's highest potential people to jump ship in an average year. These challenges are exacerbated by the growing diversity of the workforce — the talent literally "looks" different than it did a decade or two ago, and has different needs and motivations that factor into whether or not they stay with a company.

What are companies doing wrong — and how can they improve? First and foremost, the point I will keep coming back to in this book is that executives must have an active hand in all aspects of talent strategy to ensure alignment with business objectives and with the organization's entire workforce. Similarly, when it comes to talent development, don't delegate everything to frontline managers. Their involvement and accountability in setting and measuring development-related goals is critical, but many strategic assessments and decisions can only be made effectively at the executive level.

Perhaps most of all, talent strategy must be revamped with the *talent* in mind. One of the biggest mistakes corporations make is to look at talent management only from a narrow corporate standpoint. We need to also look at everything from the *employee's* point of view. Onboarding programs are a classic example. Many programs are essentially limited to checking off a set of boxes for corporate compliance. This early stage of an employee's experience with the company is a crucial opportunity to make an impression, identify personal challenges or support that will be needed, communicate the employer brand in a positive manner, and form the connections that will get someone off to a good start. When these areas are neglected, just the opposite can happen, especially with global talent — they feel like "outsiders" and question whether they are really a good fit from day one, which can become a self-fulfilling prophecy.

Similarly, it is good to customize talent management to different talent groups. As we saw in Part I of this book, today's workforce includes groups with very different values, perceptions and motives. The same approach and tactics will not work for all of them. Companies are very quick to customize products or services to sell in different markets. For example, when I was at Citibank, I saw how certain cash management products that, in the West, relied on interest, were customized to work for Eastern, Muslim cultures where "interest" was not such a central concept. The same types of adjustments can, and *should*, happen when it comes to talent management "products" and "services."

Last, but not least, one key to retaining talent is to never just "assume" that they are engaged. If emerging leaders don't get stimulating work, recognition, and the chance to prosper, they can quickly become disenchanted. (This is especially true with Millennials.) Current high performance is no guarantee of ongoing employee satisfaction or future potential. I recommend regularly evaluating talent in three areas — ability, engagement and aspiration — and then adjusting talent development accordingly.

CHAPTER 6

Refining and Retaining Your Gems

In the last chapter we looked at making talent assessment criteria more rigorous to better identify the gems who will give your company a competitive edge. We also talked about adjusting your talent strategy to better recruit and place gems coming from a wide range of backgrounds. That's just the start of course — once gems join your team, you must also do a good job of refining and retaining them. Unfulfilled potential, derailed careers, and high turnover are definitely *not* among the indicators of a high-performing organization!

When it comes to today's gems, development and retention are two more areas where a paradigm shift may be required. Specifically, the first part of this chapter will focus on restructuring career planning and development strategy by shifting from the traditional "career ladder" to a "career lattice" approach. Then we'll close the chapter by looking at how to evolve your employer brand to become more "gem-worthy."

The corporate ladder is a remnant of the Industrial Age — a once efficient, but inflexible, framework in which rewards, advancement, prestige, access to information, influence and power were strictly tied to your "level" in a vertical hierarchy. Further, the rungs on the ladder, and everything associated with them, were essentially the same for everyone.

You can probably see how this model is ill suited to almost everything we have been discussing in this book! It's not just a matter of no longer living in the Industrial Age; seismic shifts in demographics mean that the workforce is no longer uniform. Talent coming from varied backgrounds, experiences, and generations bring a wide spectrum of values and expectations in terms of what they want from their careers. But one thing that diverse groups in today's workforce *do* tend to share is a desire for more flexibility and control at work. A single linear career ladder simply doesn't align with this reality.

Similarly, recall the important trend we discussed earlier toward flatter organizational structures. Driven partly by the workforce, and partly by the nature and evolving complexity of the work itself, few organizations are structured in ways where a "ladder" fits the schema. Most are less hierarchical and more matrixed. Day-to-day work is increasingly virtual, collaborative and transparent, with information flowing quickly in many different directions. Executives must rethink career growth opportunities for their talent with all this in mind.

From both individual and organizational perspectives, another drawback of the ladder model is that it tends to focus on pushing a few select individuals up the rungs but does not adequately develop the many knowledge workers and specialists whose deep expertise, institutional knowledge, creativity and relationships are vital to daily operations and long-term success. A ladder is also harder to adapt when new skills, functions or value drivers emerge — all of which happen constantly in today's global economy! Digital technology and social media provide good examples — companies have had to develop career models for roles and skills that didn't even exist a decade ago.

If the corporate ladder's vertical growth and linear development have become obsolete, what should take its place? The best model I've seen is the "corporate lattice." As the name suggests, the corporate lattice enables work, ideas, career development and recognition to flow along multiple, intersecting paths: horizontal or diagonal as well as vertical. A lattice is a more natural fit both for the reality of the workplace and in terms of motivating today's workforce, because it facilitates more collaborative and customizable ways of structuring work and mapping career development. It is also more flexible and scalable, helping organizations adjust more quickly to the constantly shifting market landscape.

For executives, moving toward a corporate lattice model can be understood through a set of linked Awareness – Action areas:

Awareness		Action
For today's workforce, there is no universal view of success, but rather a multiplicity of desirable ways to grow and contribute		Structure organizational roles and development strategy to provide more options and emphasize that a variety of career paths and contributions are valued and supported
The emerging workforce demands better work-life balance, and the elements defining that balance vary across cultures, generations, and individuals; good work-life balance leads to better employee engagement, performance and retention		Eliminate models (and attitudes!) that pit career (high performance, ambition, productivity) and life as opposing forces; create a culture that recognizes the value of balance and supports employee priorities outside of work; put programs in place and structure Total Rewards to meet diverse work-life balance scenarios and needs
Continual, customizable professional development opportunities, both on the job and in terms of outside learning and training, are highly valued by today's top talent		Assess roles and processes with an eye toward delivering engaging, personally satisfying work experiences as well as improving productivity and efficiency; implement cost-effective professional development solutions that offer a range of opportunities for the entire workforce, not just a select few; make growth and development a measure of both individual and organizational success
Higher rates of job mobility and non-linear careers with multiple lateral/diagonal as well as vertical moves are not only becoming the norm, they have benefits for the organization as well as individuals		Embrace and facilitate cross-functional experience and expand talent development strategy to include more opportunities to learn new skills and take on roles in different areas of the company; welcome people who left the company to pursue other opportunities but want to return

I cannot emphasize enough that the benefits of a lattice structure are organizational, not just personal. Bottom-line impacts include better engagement and productivity, and lower turnover, due to improved employee satisfaction and available options to fit life into work and work into life. Some companies are even seeing reduced real estate costs as the flexibility of the lattice structure opens up opportunities to have more people work from home.

The lattice also creates agility in times of change. If someone moves on, you don't suddenly have a "missing rung" on the corporate ladder that creates obstacles and pressures; it is more likely that workflow, roles, or individual tasks can be adapted to minimize the immediate impact of the loss. Similarly, both individuals and the organization benefit from increased options for growth and development. Where the ladder only had room for a select few to advance in one direction — up — the lattice model supports continued individual growth as well as the creation of a true "learning organization" where not only careers, but also innovation and improvements, are able to move in multiple directions.

Continuing to invest in the future using an Industrial Age blueprint is futile. That's as true with talent strategy as it is with technology, marketing best practices, or any other area of business. Companies that create a corporate lattice are better positioned to attract, refine and retain a new generation of gems — and better positioned operationally as well. The lattice redefines workplace suppositions and provides a more fitting framework for the real challenges and opportunities of today's changing world of work. It is time to join other forward-looking companies in consigning the "corporate ladder" to where it belongs: in the history books.

Building a Gem-Worthy Employer Brand

I mentioned the importance of globalizing your employer brand and employer value proposition in Chapter 4. Throughout the book, there has also been a recurring emphasis on the need to assess Total Rewards strategy and programs in the context of a more diverse, multicultural workforce. But now I want to look at these important concepts in more depth. Keep in mind that, as important as your employer brand and Total Rewards may be in recruiting gems, they are even more important as fundamental touchstones that help keep *all* employees engaged, motivated and loyal.

When it comes to Total Rewards, too many companies put the cart before the horse. They roll out or redesign the Total Rewards program, then derive an employer value proposition and employer brand (if they do this formally at all) from there. The more strategic, and effective, approach is to start by asking who you are and want to be as a company, and how you are perceived and want to be perceived by your target talent. *That's* your employer brand. Within that, what central qualities differentiate you from competitors in terms of attracting, motivating and retaining your target talent? *That's* your employer value proposition. If these fundamentals aren't "clicking" for your target talent, they need to be analyzed and adjusted (in today's fast-changing environment, smart companies regularly revisit these concepts), because they influence everything else you do, from how you design your Total Rewards to what kinds of talent development programs you implement. None of this exists in a vacuum.

So — let's start by defining what we mean by "employer brand." At root, this is the market perception of what it's like to work for your company — the collective image that current and past employees and job seekers have regarding the entire employment experience at your company. Keep in mind that this may be different than your overall brand image. Unfortunately, it is not unusual for a company to invest heavily in creating and promoting a powerful brand image for consumers, investors and other stakeholders, while its employer brand goes untended and deteriorates. This represents a terrible risk. You won't be able to maintain a high-performance overall brand if your employer brand leads to a loss of talent, demotivated workforce, and inability to win top prospects.

As stressed throughout the book, the impact of human capital as a competitive differentiator is increasingly profound. To win in the marketplace, companies must find ways to differentiate themselves in attracting and retaining top talent. The qualities that do that differ depending on the industry and talent being targeted, but the bottom line is that you must have an employer brand that creates a sense of urgency and excitement about working for your company. Your products, services and overall brand are part of that, but so are the values and inclusiveness of your corporate culture, your rewards, a reputation for employee safety, care, development, whether you have a fun, challenging workplace, and much more.

When we ask why candidates should be attracted to your company and, once hired, stay with your company, the answers essentially constitute your employer value proposition (also sometimes referred to as the employee value proposition or employment value proposition). In short, what comprises the value *to the employee* of the employment experience at your company? What makes your benefits, career development opportunities, rewards, culture and workplace valuable to an employee?

To be effective, an employer value proposition must align with the company's overall brand and operational realities. The value must be authentic, and regularly reinforced by real experiences in your programs and workplaces. When that happens, the payoff is that employees — after all, the face of your company — will do a better job of delivering on their part of your overall brand promise, through productivity, innovation, quality, customer service, etc. Conversely, if the employer value proposition feels like an empty promise, employees will grow cynical, become less invested in representing your overall brand, and may eventually leave the organization entirely.

"Employee Value Propositions: Maximizing Performance Through EVP, not IOU", a short but insightful Deloitte paper on this topic, emphasizes the broader business case for investing in this area, noting that 70% of customer brand perception is determined by experiences with people (in most cases that means employees), 41% of customer loyalty can be tied to positive employee attitudes, and, on the other end of the spectrum, failure to deliver on an employer value proposition can be tied to significant drops in new hire commitment levels.[37] In other words, employee engagement, satisfaction and retention has a

---

[37] "Employee Value Propositions: Maximizing Performance Through EVP, not IOU." Deloitte Consulting, LLC. ©2010 Deloitte Development, LLC.

direct correlation with customer engagement, satisfaction and retention. When companies deliver on the employer value proposition, their employees do a better job of delivering on the overall brand promise in the market, which leads to more favorable consumer opinions, higher levels of credibility, and ultimately competitive advantage and profitability. To get the horse in front of the cart, we should *start* with the employer value proposition, not let it be an afterthought.

The most visionary companies are doing just that — proactively shaping and managing their employer value proposition (and, based on that, their Total Rewards programs) to better match their offerings with their employees' unique needs and preferences, and what they know they can consistently deliver. This more strategic approach has the added benefit of optimizing talent strategy and investment around what actually works. This is in stark contrast to less progressive peers who are constrained by out-of-date approaches to talent, including the idea that the best way to ride out an economic storm or increased competition is to *cut* investment in human capital.

Given the recent global economic recession, and continued uncertainty in many markets, this point merits further emphasis. Companies falter, and will continue faltering regardless of any economic upturn, when their programs are not in sync with the realities of their workforce. Compromising your ability to attract, engage and retain talent by looking only at where you can cut immediate costs will make it *harder* to emerge from the effects of the recession or effectively cope with inevitable market challenges and changes in the future. Navigating the complexity of global economic challenges requires just the opposite: shifting thinking away from simply reacting to the ebbs and flows of economic cycles, and instead proactively deepening your understanding of, and ability to respond to, the needs of one of your most reliable value drivers: your people. What does your workforce really value and need? The more effectively you can answer that question, the better you will attract and retain the gems who can keep your company strong through any economic cycle.

Being able to effectively answer that question also means being able to make smart choices about where to invest and where to cut in terms of what is frequently a company's largest talent spend — Total

Rewards — while preserving the power of this compelling attraction and retention centerpiece.

Let's close this chapter by looking more closely at some aspects of Total Rewards that are especially relevant to the gems we've been talking about in Part II, and to the diverse, global workforce in general. One fundamental element of Total Rewards, and a key to employee retention, is "recognition." This includes both cash and non-cash emoluments that give employees a direct incentive to do their best, and encourage high performers to stay with the company. Along with performance management and succession planning, recognition and rewards programs are closely linked to all other facets of talent management and are instrumental in supporting the company's overall business strategy and employee engagement.

However, what constitutes "recognition" and "rewards" is not an absolute; on the contrary, these concepts vary from culture to culture. One shortcoming some companies have in this area is that they apply the purely Western concept of "pay for performance" to people from cultures where it doesn't resonate. In particular, if you recall our cultural dimensions from Chapter 3, those who come from collectivist rather than individualist cultures are understandably unmotivated or confused by "recognition" that focuses almost exclusively on the individual — sometimes even to the apparent detriment of the group! In these cultures, the group is the more important entity, providing safety, support and purpose. Individuals feel a strong loyalty to the group and are motivated by what strengthens it — thus, the most appropriate recognition for such people must include praise and rewards for *group* performance.

As mentioned earlier, this is not a judgment on any culture. Each has advantages and disadvantages. Individualist cultures like the U.S. and Britain engender great individual performance, but pay the price in impaired teamwork. Collectivist cultures like Japan, India and Pakistan leverage the strength of group efforts, but pay the price in submerging individual initiative and creativity.

That brings us back to one of this book's main themes: One size does not fit all. The diverse nature of today's workforce requires greater flexibility in how recognition and rewards are defined and distributed, just as it demands a wider range of options in work arrangements and other areas.

Demographically, gems are coming more and more from Asian or Latin American backgrounds. The importance of extended family and group identity for people from these cultures is something that executives must become sensitive to and build into their policies and Total Rewards if they hope to compete for this talent.

As an example, earlier I touched on the importance of extending flex-time to help employees fulfill familial obligations. U.S. executives may not have had much direct experience with this concept in the past, but it is becoming very important as the workforce diversifies. Statistically, Asians are much more likely than Caucasians to have eldercare responsibilities: One study found that 9% of Asians have elders living with them, and 30% provide monetary support to their parents. Furthermore, they often feel guilty about the tradeoff between family care responsibilities and work, no doubt a significant factor in 63% of Asian men and 44% of Asian women reporting that they feel stalled in their careers.[38] With little prospects of realizing their ambitions, many talented and highly qualified Asians end up pulling back or exiting their companies. Now, whatever investment might be required to customize programs or create more flexible work-life balance policies, do you really want to alienate a community that is such a large economic force both inside and outside the U.S.?

The challenges that Asians face in the U.S. workforce are perhaps a subject for an entire book. But if you look at the profound impact that China and India are having on the global economy, you can see why many companies are actively invested in confronting those challenges so they can effectively tap into the Asian talent power center.

Many of the challenges are closely tied to what we've been discussing in this chapter. As an extension of talent development and recognition, for instance, one major obstacle is expecting Asians to conform to prevailing leadership models that are based entirely on a

---

[38] Hewlett, Sylvia Ann; Ripa Rashid; Claire Ho; Diana Forster. **Asians in America: Unleashing the Potential of the Model Minority.** Center for Work-Life Policy: 2011.

Western cultural ethos. This is further exacerbated by differences in communication styles, deference to authority, respect for elders, and other elements of social interaction. Some Asians find it particularly difficult to share new ideas or challenge a group consensus in a team meeting — which Westerners may misperceive as a lack of insight or initiative. Similarly, when Asian expectations of loyalty from and to managers and teams do not materialize, it can lead to low morale.

Such gaps in cultural understanding must be bridged for your company to be successful — and executives like you must take the lead in building those bridges. In Part III, I will talk more about the specifics of transforming your organization's talent initiatives and strategy. But I will close this section with a more general call to action: If we want to attract and retain the gems who can drive the company forward in a global economy, we need to *treat* them like gems and recognize that their differences *are* their value — not "difficulties" that they should give up in order to assimilate.

PART III

Taking Action to Globalize Your Talent Strategy

I began writing this book because I saw a critical need for corporate leaders to develop greater awareness of the realities of the diverse, global workforce. As "global talent" myself, some of my motivation in this area is humanistic. Certainly, I believe strongly that employees from different cultures and backgrounds should be respected and given appropriate opportunities and support to develop their skills, contribute to their organizations, and build meaningful careers.

However, as an executive and consultant, I also had strong business motivations. Globalization and demographic trends both in the U.S. and abroad have changed the workforce, and these changes will become even more profound in the years and decades ahead. Simultaneously, the value of human capital has risen to the top of the list in differentiating market competitors and defining high-performing organizations. Simply put, companies that know how to get maximum value from their workforce will thrive; those that don't — including those that ignore or mishandle the growing percentage of employees coming from other cultures and subcultures — will be in peril.

Many executives understand this on some level and have taken steps to bring their talent strategy into the 21st century. Most also understand that more needs to be done, but may be unclear about what "more" will be most effective. In some cases, good intentions are still undermined by remnants of old attitudes and assumptions, or by organizational gaps in the "cultural intelligence" that we discussed in Chapter 3. Often, this is where expertise like mine can be beneficial. If you need advice on getting the most out of global talent, it makes sense to ask someone who *is* global talent, right?

Whether I fulfill that role as an executive, consultant, adjunct professor or author, I always emphasize that we have to start with the fundamentals. Without leadership agility and a global mindset, broad cross-cultural understanding, and a culture of inclusive behavior, any policies or programs will be limited in their impact.

That said, in this last section of the book I want to move closer to the practical application of what we've learned — to what drives successful talent initiatives in Chapter 7, and then how to create a roadmap to achieve an effective global talent strategy in Chapter 8.

Of course, just as I urge executives to see that every culture, subculture and individual should be assessed on their own terms, so too, the details of talent management strategy — across acquisition, development, compensation and retention, and organizational risk — will be specific to each company's situation. Two chapters in a book do not replace the need to look at those details in depth. However, I can at least introduce some basic building blocks and leadership tips that I have found valuable for everyone in my work both as an in-house executive and as a consultant.

CHAPTER 7

Building Blocks
for Successful Talent Initiatives

To gain the competitive advantages that a diverse, global workforce can provide, it is likely that your organization will have to implement some changes. Existing talent-related programs may need to be revamped or replaced, and new programs or initiatives developed and launched. However, before diving in at the program or initiative level, it is helpful to take a step back and ask the following basic questions:

- Do we have the right mix of talent diversity? Where are our diversity "gaps"?
- How well are we fostering the continued development and retention of diverse talent? Are our programs flexible enough to adapt to cultural and generational nuances that diverse groups bring to work? If not, where do we need to improve?
- Are resources aligned appropriately to keep the talent agenda moving in the right direction? Are we anticipating future workforce make-up and needs?
- What are we doing — and where do we need to do more — to build a culture where diverse individuals can achieve their potential and different groups can collaborate successfully?

On the one hand, these are executive-level strategic questions, and the answers may well involve top-down directives, program or policy changes, or new initiatives. However, it would be a mistake to not see that answering these questions is also about what happens at the workforce level. In the most successful organizations, diverse groups in the workforce all feel liberated and empowered to take risks, engage, and contribute *their* ideas to programs and policies. In other words, the advice here is to involve the talent in talent-related program assessments and decisions! Not only does this make employees feel valued, driving engagement and retention, it also ensures that you have the input necessary to "get it right." Particularly with a multicultural workforce, if programs don't incorporate the ideas and perspectives of the different groups impacted, there is a high risk that they will be based on incomplete or incorrect assumptions and therefore be ineffective.

This brings us back to the important distinction between organizational learning and a learning organization. Organizational learning is programmatic; for example, you might have a diversity and inclusion course that all employees take, or related training modules that correspond to certain roles or stages in the employee development cycle. This is all fine, but to achieve a high-performing, diverse workplace, training courses are not enough. You must also establish a learning organization — a culture where everyone is constantly learning. That can only happen if people are allowed, and encouraged, to take risks, and make and learn from mistakes. It requires a commitment to open, respectful dialogue, and an avoidance of the sort of "blame culture" where everyone's focus tends to be on assigning or avoiding blame.

A learning organization has enormous advantages when it comes to leveraging a diverse, multicultural workforce. Cultural understanding and inclusive behavior become a natural, everyday manifestation, not just something covered in a training course or touched on briefly during quarterly department meetings. Just as importantly, because challenges and mistakes are embraced as opportunities to learn and improve, overall cultural intelligence constantly expands and there is less chance of a one-time misunderstanding resulting in longer-term resentment or confusion. In short, the "risks" of greater diversity are mitigated, while the benefits in terms of innovation and complementary collaboration are fully unleashed! Further, a learning culture is one of the essential "pull factors" that define you as a leading employer brand that can attract the global talent gems we talked about in Part II.

In essence, building a learning organization is a people-centric rather than program-centric approach. Similarly, whether we're talking about launching a leadership diversity initiative or redesigning your Total Rewards strategy, today's talent landscape makes a people-centric approach the only effective one.

Consider the multiple generations in today's workforce for example. No single "program approach" will work equally well for World War II, Baby Boomer, Generation X and Millennial generations — they are too different! Generation X and Millennials seek different outcomes from work, expect greater input and flexibility in determining how and where work is done, and respond to different motivations than prior generations. With Generation X, developing relationships is a key to retention; although goal-oriented, they have less need for performance feedback. Millennials are more independent and confident, but also have a sociability that leads them to favor collective action. As "digital natives," technology is essential to how they learn and communicate. They are also highly motivated by work-life balance — to retain them, you must assure that they can maintain a personal life.

The list of differences could go on and on. And generations are a relatively simple case compared to the diversity of cultures and subcultures in the workforce. A program or incentive to motivate someone from talent power centers in Asia or Latin America may need to be quite different from what has traditionally been used with U.S. workers. Bottom line, with any program or strategy involving talent, it has become essential to take it to the "people" level and factor in the different values and needs throughout the workforce.

Let's take a fresh look at Total Rewards and Integrated Talent Management strategy to see how this plays out. From a people-centric perspective, the first thing to note is that, for a broad range of groups, compensation, benefits and wellness programs are now an expected "baseline." By themselves, they are not likely to differentiate your organization in competing for talent. How *will* you differentiate? A people-centric approach — including inviting employee and prospective candidate participation in designing the Total Rewards program structure — can help illuminate compelling, forward-looking options.

For example, people-centric means looking at how you can support employee decisions and behaviors that impact the value of benefits. So, instead of just contributing to your employees' retirement funds —

now a "baseline" benefit — the differentiator might be providing onsite financial guidance and proven, data-driven tools that help employees improve their financial behavior and achieve greater, more enduring prosperity. Another option to boost "retirement readiness" could be counseling or training that prepares employees for part-time jobs, investment management and other activities that may constitute a "career after their career."

The key to people-centric talent programs goes back to what we've talked about throughout this book: asking (and asking your people) whether programs and policies truly align with the increasingly diverse needs of today's talent. Answering that question should be a central concern in every area, starting with ensuring that managers understand, respect and are able to adapt to the dramatically different work styles, expectations, motivators, performance goals, personal-time needs and cultural norms of the contemporary workforce.

At the program level, one good example of a more people-centric approach is to implement strategic employee recognition programs that enable you to *customize* rewards to appeal to the diverse interests of different generations, cultures and subcultures. Offering employees their "rewards of choice" can help you win talent and stimulate morale, engagement and productivity across a wider spectrum of needs and interests. For some, the most valuable reward for their hard work and contributions might be the ability to work remotely, or greater flexibility for family leave than standard FMLA covers, or opportunities to develop their talent that are not limited to narrow organizational objectives, or extra amenities like daycare or free onsite meals and services.

Taking a people-centric approach exposes you directly to the realities of your people. In most workforces, that means higher percentages of women, Asians and Latin Americans, making it vital to redesign Total Rewards and Integrated Talent Management strategy to fit these affinity groups. For example, we know that women are entering the workforce at higher rates than men, and that significant numbers of them are working moms or single moms. Attracting and retaining top talent from this grow-ing pool requires offering them greater flexibility to manage and balance personal and work life, as well as developing leadership programs that are women-centric and help them break through the "glass ceiling."

A people-centric talent strategy is closely entwined with another concept mentioned throughout this book: reverse acculturation. It's hard to align programs with diverse talent unless executives are willing to put themselves in the "other's" shoes and develop a deeper understanding of the different values and needs that "outside" talent groups bring to the workplace. That personal commitment is a necessary first step, but now let's explore some organizational goals and tips that will help you move from good intentions to an authentically supportive, learning organization where inclusive behavior is the norm and talent from all backgrounds can flourish.

Align Organizational Values With Workforce Values

A diverse, global workforce brings a wide range of values to the workplace. That makes it all the more important to have *organizational* values that resonate with and can unify different groups and individuals. It is also worth noting that some of the fastest-growing workforce groups, particularly Millennials, are more attracted to values-based organizations that exhibit a real commitment to social responsibility and good corporate citizenship.

Volunteer and service programs can be especially effective in this area, because they "walk the talk" and make values tangible and shareable on a regular basis. Organizing and supporting volunteer opportunities, including potentially providing flex-time to pursue them, aiding employees in fundraising campaigns, and so on, is an excellent way to show the organization's commitment to helping the community. Just as importantly, volunteering allows multiple generations and cultures to come together for common goals outside of their work responsibilities.

Corporate Culture 2.0: Replace Conformity With Inclusive Behavior

In the current work environment, which is vastly more diverse than even 10 years ago, efforts to maintain a cohesive corporate identity through cultural conformity and pressure to assimilate are bound to fail. The concept of a monolithic corporate culture that transcends, or takes precedence over, one's personal culture has become obsolete and out of tune with the demands of today's talent. Global commerce, migration flows, sociocultural realities, technology that enables instant communication around the world — these and other forces make it clear that the only way forward is to encourage and embrace diverse expression and multicultural differences *as* the new defining qualities of a dynamically evolving corporate culture.

As discussed in Chapter 4, this goes far beyond just hiring a more diverse workforce, or complying with diversity-related regulations or targets. This is about transforming attitudes, expectations and management styles so that the central priority becomes promoting inclusive behavior instead of demanding "corporate culture conformity." Accepting the reality of cultural *non*-conformity in the workplace is the essential first step toward tapping the enormous benefits of diverse and complementary talent, including the potential for breakthrough insights, dynamic learning and innovation, and a more natural alignment with diverse, global markets. In short, creating a culture of inclusive behavior that will attract diverse, global talent isn't a humanistic concern, it's a strategic imperative.

Develop Leadership Styles (and Leaders) That Fit Your Talent

In the past, the focus of "developing a leadership style" was often almost entirely on the individual leader, with the goal being to "find your own leadership style." Workforce diversity, as well as changing expectations about relationships between the "leaders" and the "led," have turned that paradigm upside down. The most effective leaders today are those who are agile enough to adapt leadership styles to a range of different individuals and situations. The question for senior executives has become how to identify and develop leaders who have this agility, and how to help them develop cross-cultural intelligence and become adept at managing, motivating, and communicating with talent from diverse backgrounds.

Based on my experience with some of the world's top organizations, including Citigroup, National Citibank (now PNC), Ameriprise Financial, American Red Cross, and Amtrak, I have seen many different types of leaders ultimately succeed in working with diverse, global talent. However, the one thing they all have in common is what I've returned to again and again in this book: reverse acculturation. To be effective in the 21st century business environment, leaders must be willing and able to learn about, respect, and appreciate the unique value of "others" who are different from them — whether that difference is national, racial, ethnic, gender, generational, sexual orientation, religious tradition, or anything else. Similarly, the most effective leadership hiring and development programs I've seen make it a priority for leaders to become sensitive to the impact of the cultural nuances, perspectives, and ideas that diverse employees bring with them to the workplace.

Put More "Total" in Total Rewards Programs and Structures

Total Rewards is an area that executives truly must address if they hope to attract and retain the best and brightest regardless of national origin, age, race, gender, cultural background, and so on. Traditional Total Rewards offerings based on compensation and benefits must be expanded and reinvented. No matter how competitive you may be on straight compensation and benefits, you will lose valuable talent if you don't also pay attention to other "rewards" that today's employees value.

One obvious area that needs to be included is schedule flexibility. Whether to help a family member in need, take care of children, balance a long commute, or pursue meaningful volunteer or avocational activities, many employees are looking for flex-time, work-from-home options, and other solutions that can help them fulfill outside obligations and achieve good work-life balance. Another area that should be on the top of any initiative list is providing accessible, meaningful personal and professional development opportunities. Millennials in particular are looking for organizations that will invest in their development and offer the potential for rapid career growth and visibility.

It is also important to look at how Total Rewards, including development opportunities, are playing out for specific groups. For example, the growing number of women in the workplace are specifically targeting organizations with a track record of selecting and promoting women into the C-suite and onto Boards of Directors.

To put it simply, Total Rewards programs need to offer something that genuinely rewards every group in the workforce. If there are gaps in Total Rewards, there will be gaps in the talent that you are able to attract and retain.

Question the Performance of Your Performance Management

When we talk about reinventing the Total Rewards structure, one component — performance management — merits special attention, both because of its overall competitive impact and because of the special challenges it presents in the context of a diverse, global workforce. In assessing how performance is gauged and rewarded, executives have to be particularly cognizant of the fact that the performance management system that is appropriate for Western cultures does not work as well in other cultures. As noted earlier, concepts such as "pay for performance" evolved out of individualist American and Western European (Dutch) cultures and don't make as much sense to people from collectivist cultures where "group success" takes priority over individual achievement. If you're looking to performance as a competitive differentiator, you'll need to create a performance management system that actually works for the full range of employees.

Interestingly, even the concept of "performance management" has become a subject of debate in the U.S. — with some organizations deciding that traditional performance management approaches widely adopted over the past two decades are now passé. The fundamental question being asked is whether such systems add enough value to offset fissures in the organization caused by employees (sometimes high percentages of employees) disgruntled by how their performance is gauged and rewarded. REI, Microsoft and others have decided to fully or partially move away from performance management, particularly the use of stack or forced rankings.

Whether or not companies keep or abandon their performance management process in general, what is evident is that we all have to align how we manage, gauge, monitor and motivate performance with the realities of today's workforce. Likewise, if a company has a global presence, the performance management system should be flexible enough to adapt to the regional market environments and varied cultures where the workforce operates.

What is also evident is that executives cannot simply take an existing system as scripture — or expect it to be treated that way. It's necessary to ask, in today's environment, whether a system is really driving engagement and performance and providing talent decision-making criteria. Or — is it just training people to check the right boxes and regurgitate prescribed phrases? If it's the latter, it's time for a new system, no matter what the makeup of your workforce may be.

Leader-Led Development

According to research conducted by the Corporate Executive Board, the "rising leaders" who report to the most effective senior leaders perform up to 27% better, their teams work harder, and the senior leaders themselves are 50% more likely to exceed their financial goals.[39] To facilitate this, consider a "leader-led development" initiative to map out an ongoing, dynamic series of job-related interactions that match a senior leader and rising leader, with the purpose of improving the latter's performance and readiness for future leadership roles. Such an initiative offers additional value in terms of opportunities to support diverse, global talent throughout the leadership pipeline, and to ensure that *all* future leaders are encouraged to develop the agility and cultural intelligence so vital to leading tomorrow's workforce.

A critical prerequisite to succeeding with this model is to make sure senior leaders have access to the resources necessary to impact the rising leader's performance, such as training and coaching. This is another area where cultural sensitivity and customization is vital. The types of training and coaching that work well with many rising leaders in the U.S. may not be effective or sufficient for a rising leader from China or India or Brazil.

Across all cultures, there are six qualities of successful leader-led development relationships that an initiative should encourage and gauge to ensure success. Three of these qualities govern the tone and focus of the senior leader in relation to the rising leader:

- Respectful, fair treatment
- Leadership vision and inspiration
- Credibility in effective management of the business and overall leadership skills

---

[39] "Leaders Who Develop Leaders: Strategies for Effective Leader-Led Development." Corporate Executive Board: 2006.

The other three qualities apply to the rising leader in relationship to the senior leader:
- Positive relationship and perception
- Comfort taking the initiative
- Eagerness to learn, including embracing opportunities to learn from mistakes

Both individuals must strive to embody all three qualities on their side of the relationship to ensure the most valuable development experience and outcome. Senior leaders should also keep in mind that they lead by example; if they demonstrate a real commitment to their own development, it sends a potent message to rising leaders. It also contributes significantly to establishing the kind of learning culture or learning organization that we talked about earlier.

People Management

Having and communicating an inspiring vision for your organization is uniquely important in guiding it to future success. However, vision alone isn't enough. The "flame" of vision will go awry or sputter out altogether if it is not carried forward and fueled by your employees. In other words, we arrive once again at the central role of human capital and, consequently, the importance of "people management" strategies and programs that align with the workforce. A diverse, global workforce requires programs that are flexible enough to resonate with different cultures and subcultures. However, I want to touch on the three qualities — empowerment, loyalty and professional stake — that are essential to all people management efforts.

In Chapter 1's discussion about the trend toward decentralization, I identified **empowerment** as the "leg" managers sometimes forget to attach to a three-legged stool that also includes accountability and responsibility. The resulting imbalance often prevents employees from fully contributing and undermines overall performance. A good people management approach doesn't merely encourage or evaluate employees in their ability to take initiative or make decisions — it *empowers* them to do so by giving them the tools, training, support (including cultural support), and, importantly, the decision-making authority, that they need. Empowerment is the key that unlocks creative thinking, innovation, productivity, outstanding service, and higher performance in almost every area where people are involved in the outcomes.

A second aspect of people management, **loyalty**, has shifted significantly over the past couple decades. With the current workforce, it is insufficient for managers to "expect" employee loyalty; in fact, the expectation itself can undermine the desired result. Loyalty simply cannot be a one-sided affair anymore. To earn and sustain employee loyalty, it is equally critical for the organization and its managers to *show* loyalty to staff — from ensuring fair treatment and appropriate rewards, to taking measures to protect jobs during a downturn, to providing allowances for employee errors and omissions and treating them as learning opportunities rather than cause for punitive action. An organization that *gives* loyalty will get loyalty — and also benefit from positive market reputation, ability to attract top talent, and the kinds of frontline attitudes and behaviors that will result in greater productivity and cost-containment.

As someone from an Eastern, collectivist culture, I have a unique perspective on why loyalty often seems to fall short in U.S. corporations. Going back to the cultural dimensions of Hofstede and Trompenaars, the U.S. has a very individualist orientation. This plays out in two ways that tend to negatively impact loyalty. First, success here is often defined and rewarded primarily, or even exclusively, in terms of individual accomplishment — whereas loyalty, by definition, involves valuing a relationship to others or to a group. For all the lip service that is paid to loyalty, if the day-to-day reality is that it isn't a priority and doesn't get recognized or rewarded, then we shouldn't be surprised if employees do not develop this quality.

A second observation in regard to loyalty is that U.S. business culture is often much more influenced by market dynamics than other cultures — with enormous focus on short-term performance and goals (e.g., quarterly earnings) as a driver of strategy. If earnings fall below "Wall Street expectations," there is typically an immediate move to cut costs, with the workforce being the first target. Since labor-related costs are among an organization's greatest expenses, this can indeed be a "quick fix," but it is also a short-sighted one that may undermine organizational performance down the road. After all, you can hardly expect loyalty from employees if they always bear the burden in a downturn. The resulting lack of loyalty will translate into higher turnover costs, lower morale and productivity, potential gaps in institutional knowledge and other negatives. This phenomenon is not common in cultures like Pakistan, China, India, Brazil, South Africa, and others where loyalty has high cultural importance and a multiplicity of personal bonds are forged in the workplace with leadership as well as peers. As a result, turnover and employee mobility are much lower, and common U.S. practices like "headhunting" and luring away employees with a short-term raise or bonus, are still rare.

A third component of good people management involves giving employees a **professional stake** — in other words, making it clear how organizational goals or achievements will answer the question, "What's in it for me?" Here, I always encourage executives to go beyond the traditional confines of pay and benefits. These are *not* the only way to attract and retain talent. On the contrary, for today's talent, a professional stake may be defined by opportunities for development, career mobility, reward and recognition, work-life balance, a congenial and satisfying work environment, the chance to do work that aligns with their values, and much more.

*　　*　　*　　*　　*

As a consultant, when executives ask my opinion about why a past talent program or initiative was ineffective or failed to deliver the desired outcomes, I am always quick to raise certain questions: Were your people at the center of the program or initiative? Was the program or initiative designed with their needs in mind? Did you get input from the people, or at least types of people, that the program or initiative was supposed to attract or help? Did the program or initiative take into account differences in the workforce related to culture, gender, race, generation and sexual orientation? Did the program have an active and visible leadership commitment or sponsorship?

All of these questions essentially boil down to whether or not the talent strategy is people-centric. To be people-centric is to notice, honor and respond to differences *in* your people. It is when we are too focused on everything *other* than our people that we tend to miss those differences and make decisions that undermine our good intentions.

Of course, even if you are confident about having a people-centric approach and embodying the talent management qualities discussed in this chapter, there is still the matter of pulling everything together into a formal strategy and action plan. And that takes us to our final chapter.

CHAPTER 8

Leading the Way to
a Winning Talent Strategy

When I chose this book's subtitle — *What CEOs, Boards and Management Teams Must Learn and Do to Win With a Diverse, Global Workforce* — I wanted to identify my intended audience, but also evoke the reality faced by most U.S.-based corporations. Competing in a global economy, including attracting and leveraging global talent, requires change — and change requires strong leadership and active involvement at the top of the organization.

Talent strategy should not be an afterthought or something developed in an HR silo and then rubber-stamped by the board of directors. On the contrary, a key point I have emphasized throughout this book is that talent strategy must be aligned with (and should also influence) top-level business strategy. Further, the resulting talent agenda must be supported by appropriate resources to drive organizational performance. That's not just funding new initiatives, or hiring the right HR executives, or allocating the budget to support a strong Total Rewards program. All of those are critical of course, but so is the visible involvement of top executives throughout the organization. Particularly when it comes to change challenges like building a diversity-respecting culture of inclusive behavior, the rest of the organization will follow the example set by senior leaders. If they are actively invested in the change, that sets the tone for the entire workforce.

When a board or executive team brings me in with the goal of better leveraging talent to spur or sustain growth and competitive advantage in the global marketplace, I start by framing our task within the larger picture of creating and pursuing a change agenda. That agenda should include talent strategy at both a macro level (organizational culture/ change) and micro level (specific programs or domains). To succeed, macro and micro strategies must align and resonate with the diverse cultural makeup of today's workforce — and, just as importantly, anticipate what that workforce will look like, need, and be motivated by in the years ahead.

Let's look more closely at how this plays out on both the macro and micro levels, and then I will close the book with a few thoughts on executive action plans.

Talent Strategy at the Macro Level

At the macro level, I want to hone in on an important strategic objective I've discussed previously: creating a learning organization. Although most organizations design, fund and implement a wide range of programs geared toward developing talent, too often the focus is solely on "organizational learning" — formal training and developmental processes that cover everything from role-specific knowledge to competency areas and leadership skills up to organization-wide compliance courses. However, by itself, organizational learning is not adequate to address all of your business challenges and needs. In today's fast-paced, culturally diverse environments, it is essential to also create a "learning organization" or "learning culture."

At many companies, this is often the missing piece that hasn't been given enough attention. In a learning organization, learning isn't limited to the classroom or online courses or leadership development seminars. On the contrary, it is ongoing and everywhere, a natural part of daily activity. Perhaps most importantly, in a learning organization, there is a focus at all levels on learning from failures. This requires a fundamental shift in mindset for some leaders in that talent must be allowed (or even encouraged) to make mistakes without retribution. But, if continuous learning and improvement are strategic goals — and they should be — then mistakes should be treated as golden opportunities to advance those goals.

The payoff in establishing a learning culture is tremendous. Learning organizations become skilled at continuously creating, acquiring and transferring knowledge throughout the organization, and at modifying behaviors to reflect new insights and environmental conditions.

They facilitate more systematic problem solving, as well as the experimentation with new approaches that drives successful innovation. All of these attributes are vital for becoming a high-performing organization and gaining a competitive advantage in the marketplace.

Senior leaders have a pivotal role to play both in making the establishment of a learning organization a strategic objective and in demonstrating their own commitment to behaviors that help create a climate where a learning culture can flourish. For example:

- **Encourage inclusive behavior and actively invite the input and participation of diverse groups and individuals throughout the workforce.** This is not only critical to establishing a learning organization, it is becoming a practical necessity due to the increasing diversity in the workforce. You simply can't afford to have growing employee demographics like women, racial and ethnic minorities, immigrants, and physically challenged workers feel that they are excluded from decision-making or that they must suppress their differences. On the contrary, the different perspectives and insights they bring to the workplace are precisely what can help you attain a competitive advantage.

- **Embrace reverse acculturation.** One of this book's key themes bears repeating once more, because, in a diverse, multicultural workplace, reverse acculturation is essential to establishing a learning culture. Leaders set the tone; rather than expecting your workforce to conform to your (or to a narrowly defined corporate) culture, practice and preach the value of reverse acculturation. Make a concerted effort to understand and appreciate cultures that are different from your own. Embracing employees from other backgrounds provides the benefits of the different cultural lens they bring to the workplace. Reverse acculturation also exposes leaders to cultural nuances that can provide valuable insight into successful approaches for new and emerging markets.

- **Facilitate and reward team learning.** In an individualistic culture like the U.S., establishing a true learning culture is sometimes constrained by the fact that learning priorities, programs and rewards tend to revolve around the individual. This leaves many learning opportunities untapped at the team level, and can lead to an environment where some individuals have motives to embrace the "learning culture" model, but others do not. Leaders must emphasize (and demonstrate) that learning from mistakes, and continuous improvement, should happen at every level. One way to reinforce that message is to tie at least some rewards to team-related performance outcomes and behaviors.

- **Clearly integrate talent development requirements with business goals.** Strategic prioritization and investment tell the entire workforce what truly matters to leadership, and, by extension, what should matter to each worker. Talent development, including the support and processes that help create a learning culture, will not arise spontaneously — there must be executive-level planning, commitment and promotion. Aligned with strategic business needs, this should manifest as investment in specific areas of process, technology and people. (More on this in the next section.)

- **Identify key competencies needed to drive short-term and long-term business strategies.** Prioritizing and investing in the development of key competencies delivers immediate business value, helps improve corporate bench strength and, at the culture level, reinforces a "learning" mindset. It is important to differentiate needed competencies, and then ask: Which competencies are served by existing development resources? Which need additional investment? What maturity level is needed for leaders to take on higher-level competencies?

- **Continuously monitor internal/external environmental trends and the competitive business landscape.** This is good advice in general, but it also parallels the basic "learning culture" model, which is about constantly scanning the environment for ways to learn and improve. The point here is twofold. First, constant environmental scans at the executive level will turn up learning and improvement opportunities that can be funneled to appropriate parts of the organization. Second, this models, at a senior level, the mindset and behavioral orientation you want practiced company-wide.

- **Encourage utilization of information technology.** The latest information technology can't cover *all* learning, development and information-sharing needs, but it can be a tremendous enabling tool in many areas.

Micro Level: Roadmap to Transform the Talent Strategy

The micro level of talent strategy can be broken down into eight domains. For each, an organization should map out its existing state, desired state, and path to transformation via the levers of process, people and technology. Taken together, the talent domain tables that follow comprise a roadmap that a company's leaders would use to evolve each domain to drive better performance and achieve top-level business objectives. Again, the content of a roadmap like this, particularly the process/people/technology section, will vary from company to company. Consider this a template, populated with general, high-level advice to help illustrate the approach, and hopefully spark insights as to its applicability and value for your organization.

Talent Domain: Alignment to Enterprise

FROM	TO	HOW
Lacking Strategic Alignment * Talent management not aligned to strategic execution of corporate goals * Reactionary responses to talent needs	**Driving Enterprise Value** * Talent aligned to strategic goals * Talent viewed as change catalysts who facilitate innovation and improvement initiatives that will drive organizational performance	*Process: Align business goals and processes with the talent strategy, not the other way around* *People: Get to know your talent by creating talent intelligence resumes and revisiting them regularly* *Technology/Systems: Share data on customer satisfaction and financial performance with employees, especially areas that are weaknesses vis-à-vis the competition*

Talent Domain: Investment

FROM	TO	HOW
Insufficient Investment to Support Talent Needs * Lack of investment in the processes, programs and technology to gauge talent gaps and provide appropriate solutions	**Enterprise-Level Investment Supporting Talent Needs** * Business strategy drives enterprise investments to support talent needs through people and technological systems * Economies of scale and enhanced return on investment	***Process:*** *During budgetary cycle, investment in the talent strategy should be present from the start, not an afterthought; similarly, in a downturn don't let this be the first or only area subject to reductions in budget allocation* ***People:*** *Invest capital in talent's developmental needs as aligned with achieving short- and long-term business goals, as well as identifying opportunities to leverage the talent in a business downturn* ***Technology/Systems:*** *Integrate talent management and Total Rewards systems through a single platform to drive greater interoperability and align talent needs delivery*

Talent Domain: Talent Acquisition

FROM	TO	HOW
Recruitment Planning * Administrative and transactional focus	**Strategic Workforce Development** * Identifying and successfully addressing talent gaps through strategic workforce development	***Process:*** *Shift focus from recruitment planning to strategic workforce planning* ***People:*** *Identify future skills required for the business and hire and/or develop employees along those skill sets* ***Technology/Systems:*** *Develop analytic tools to gauge talent gap risks and drive fact-based business decisions with insights from talent metrics*

Talent Domain: Knowledge Management

FROM	TO	HOW
Redundancies * Knowledge-sharing silos creating redundancies in programs, ineffective management styles and talent development	**Collaborative Culture Empowered by Deliberate Knowledge Management** * Empowering talent, providing it with excellence and promoting partnerships, strategy execution, and innovation	*Process: Think globally, not limited to the uses of knowledge management in your division or geography; mine its broader value across the enterprise, and treat it as a corporate initiative, not just a department-focused solution* *People: Institutionalize process enabling knowledge transfer from retiring workforce to newer hires; incent retirees to act as coaches, mentors and subject matter experts to bridge knowledge gaps* *Technology/Systems: Use social media as a vehicle for knowledge management strategy*

Talent Domain: Culture of Accountability

FROM	TO	HOW
Hard Work, But Unmeasured Results * Performance outcome tied to job description * Significant effort expended on "getting things done" but no clear definition of success or metrics to show what has been accomplished	**Smart Work Delivering SMART Outcomes** * Performance specifications determining and measuring talent deliverables * Focus on effectiveness, quality, and efficiency through measuring the programs, service delivery, and strategic use of resources	*Process: Stop measuring sub-unit performance based only on narrow functional goals; set revenue, income, productivity, customer satisfaction, and cycle-time targets so high that they can't be reached by conducting business as usual* *People: Insist that more people be held accountable for broad measures of business performance in addition to core job accountability* *Technology/Systems: Provide greater transparency on customer service and business performance data, especially as it demonstrates weaknesses vis-à-vis competitors*

Talent Domain: Talent Management and Development

FROM	TO	HOW
Limited Professional Development * Talent gap and inadequate resources devoted to strategic workforce development programs * "Career ladder" focused on linear development and narrow set of candidates	**Enhanced Training and Career Opportunities** * Strong focus on programs to improve workforce engagement and performance * Growth opportunities for talent across the enterprise * "Career lattice" that facilitates lateral and diagonal as well as vertical moves and opens development opportunities to broad range of talent	*Process: Define critical career paths first; align with core and technical competencies and then with tailored development paths* *People: Develop people through robust succession planning with opportunities for cross-functional exposure; expand talent assessment to include Differentiator and Best-Fit criteria, not just High-Potential or High-Performer* *Technology/Systems: Distinguish between critical and core roles; develop role progression and identify opportunities for movement in the profession*

Talent Domain: Total Rewards

FROM	TO	HOW
Retrenched, Old Ideas * Narrow focus on managing costs, particularly in order to "ride out the economic storm" * Vanilla compensation and benefits programs that do not differentiate in the marketplace	**Define Employer Value Proposition (EVP) and Align With Brand** * Create and leverage compelling EVP and employer brand promise * Reinvent Total Rewards to better align with needs and motivations of today's workforce	*Process: Integrate Talent Strategy with Total Rewards Program* *People: Create and align EVP to address needs of a diverse workforce* *Technology/Systems: Harness the power of social media platforms to market EVP and enhance and leverage the power of the employer brand*

Talent Domain: Change Management

FROM	TO	HOW
Focus on Project Implementation * Lacking alignment with behavioral change	**Focus on Three Pillars of Effective Change Management** * Leadership * Project management plan * Change management plan	*Process: Provide the vision leading to the preparation for change; manage the change process; reinforce change behaviors by aligning them with incentives* *People: Have leadership provide sponsorship, not only in name, but by actively and visibly leading change agenda* *Technology/Systems: Identify one methodology for change and stick with it; ensure that it becomes the organizational protocol*

Executive Action Plan

I hope this book has increased your motivation to confront the challenges, and begin reaping the incredible value, of global talent. If so, you may be thinking about next steps such as developing an executive action plan. To lay the groundwork for that, I suggest first assessing where your organization falls on the spectrum between high-performing and low-performing companies, particularly in relation to how you respond to organizational talent. Once again, i4cp provides excellent guidance in where to look...and why these areas merit action. Consider the following findings from their 2010 *Organizational and Leadership Agility Survey* report. Compared to low-performing companies, the report notes that high-performing companies are:

- 7x as effective at managing learning and development
- 5x as effective at leadership development, coaching and recognition
- 4x as effective at building and managing teams, aging of the workforce and building compensation strategies for different workforce segments

- 3x as effective at succession planning, performance management, measuring human capital, compensation, managing the global workforce, multicultural teams and outsourcing HR
- 2x as effective at managing/coping with change and organizational change, workforce analytics, workforce planning, measuring/rewarding behavior, internal communication, retention, skill level of the workforce, strategy development, building (or rebuilding) the employer brand, global economic situation, quality of life, healthcare management, corporate restructuring, generations at work, diversity and inclusion, benefits, mergers and acquisitions, and global health threats[40]

Clearly, significant differences across all areas of talent strategy and management distinguish high-performers from low-performers. I will add that this becomes a virtuous cycle — excellence in these areas attracts top talent and drives performance, which further improves the talent management function just as it improves other business areas. The path to that virtuous cycle starts with executive leadership as well as your HR talent. Given the many workplace changes over the past decade, and the continuing diversification of the workforce in particular, it is wise to assess your HR function and internal HR talent to determine how well positioned you are to formulate and execute a truly effective, global talent strategy. Are your HR leaders asking the right questions?

- Is our company focused on the top leading talent strategy issues, such as strategy alignment and execution, retention, talent acquisition, talent management and workforce planning?
- Is our company honing in on competencies that correlate with market performance, such as global

---

[40] *Organizational and Leadership Agility Survey.* Also available online at www.i4cp.com/productivity-blog/2010/03/11/agile-leaders-generate-greater-corporate-performance. Institute for Corporate Productivity, Inc.: 2010.

mindset, organizational change and design, strategy development and execution?

- Is our company creating a differentiated talent force capable of delivering superior innovation and creativity, sustainability, and global market penetration?
- Is our company doing all it can to measure and increase the value of human capital?
- Is our company differentiating pay and Total Rewards to attract and retain top talent?
- Is our company utilizing workforce analytics to help make informed and judicious decisions on our most valuable asset — *people*?

Unfortunately, many companies are not asking the right questions, do not have the internal expertise or experience with diverse, global talent to come up with the right answers, and rely on outdated talent paradigms that become more and more ineffective with each passing year. The need for executives, boards and management teams to understand and address this is what inspired me to begin writing this book. It is also a central value of my consulting firm. In many cases, external expertise and support like ours may be the most effective and timely way to get your talent strategy on track to high-performance.

However, this book is not about trying to drum up consulting work. The competitive realities of the global marketplace, combined with the fact that human capital has taken center stage as a value driver and differentiator in most industries, mean you simply can't afford to be an underperformer when it comes to talent.

Because of my unique background as both global talent and an executive who has worked with several large, U.S.-based global organizations, I feel a personal connection and motivation in helping both sides of the equation. I want global talent to be respected and given the proper environment to excel. I also want executives in my adopted country to get the value from global talent that they need to be competitive in the global economy.

That can only happen if we commit to developing a new global talent paradigm that transforms everything from mindsets and management styles up to development initiatives and Total Rewards structure. It will not always be an easy journey, but we have much to gain by making it: smoother running, higher-performing organizations, stronger competitive position and greater profitability, and happier employees who are better able to realize their full potential.

ACKNOWLEDGEMENTS

I would like to acknowledge and thank the many friends and colleagues who over the past several years have encouraged me to write this book — and many more who have inspired me throughout my career. I am also deeply grateful to the numerous senior leaders that I have had the distinct pleasure of working with over the past two decades. Their example gave me confidence that the material in this book would be well received and could lead to dynamic positive organizational changes.

I would also like to thank Geert Hofstede and Fons Trompenaars for allowing me to draw on their rich scholarly research and literature as I shaped the direction of this book. They have been extremely gracious and generous in allowing me to reference their research findings throughout this book.

Finally, I would like to express my gratitude to my editor Don Bertschman, who accompanied me through the entire journey of writing this book, talking over ideas, reading drafts and offering comments, and editing the manuscript from start to finish. Realizing the vision I had for this book would not have been possible without his focus and diligence.

Made in the USA
Charleston, SC
18 April 2014